How to
Make Your
Training
Pay

To
Mandy Little and her colleagues at Watson, Little Ltd

How to Make Your Training Pay

HOW TO WRING EVERY DROP OF VALUE FROM YOUR TRAINING BUDGET

MALCOLM BIRD

BUSINESS BOOKS LIMITED

First published in Great Britain in 1991 by
Business Books Limited
An imprint of Random Century Limited
20 Vauxhall Bridge Road, London SW1V 2SA

Random Century Australia (Pty) Limited
20 Alfred Street, Milsons Point, Sydney
New South Wales 2061, Australia

Random Century New Zealand Limited
9–11 Rothwell Avenue, Albany, Glenfield
Auckland 10, New Zealand

Random Century South Africa (Pty) Limited
PO Box 337, Bergvlei, South Africa

Set in 12/13 Monophoto Garamond by
Servis Filmsetting, Limited, Manchester, England

Printed and bound in Great Britain by
MacKays of Chatham PLC, Chatham, Kent

British Library Cataloguing in Publication Data
A catalogue record for this book is available
from the British Library

ISBN 0-7126-5015-6

CONTENTS

ACKNOWLEDGEMENTS

I am grateful to Katy Eyre, Managing Director of Jacoranda Production Limited for valuable advice and information on commissioning a training video.
I am also indebted to K.W. Mortimer of the Ford Motor Company Limited for supplying details of the Ford EDAP scheme and to Susan Bishop of Macmillan Intek Limited for an explanation of the nature and use of Macmillan Intek training packages and programmes.

FOREWORD

HOW DO YOU and your company regard training?

Do you see it as an investment for the future and as a way to increase profits – or do you see it as something to go along with just to keep the Personnel Manager happy?

Your company – like many others – may do no training of its employees at all.

Some companies 'justify' their lack of training with statements such as:

- If we train them they will leave for a higher paid job elsewhere
- We recruit ready trained people
- We have no time for training – we are all too busy
- We cannot afford the cost of training
- No-one here needs training.

Or, simply 'What is the point in spending time and money on training?'

There is another side to this coin. There are companies who are committed to training because 'it is a GOOD THING'. These are the people who spend time and money on satisfying a 'textbook' requirement for training with little or no real idea why they are doing it.

One such company has a policy that all its employees will receive 15 days training each year. No doubt the original intention was a good one but it has deteriorated to the point where almost any old training will do as long as each person clocks up his or her 15 days.

This approach not only brings serious training into disrepute but also costs a lot of money.

These various attitudes are examined in this book but the emphasis will be on showing you how you and your company can benefit from training. However small or large your organization may be, properly planned and organized training can enhance profits or, in extreme cases, make the difference between failure and survival.

The masculine gender has been used throughout and, unless the context otherwise indicates, both sexes are implied. This is to relieve the tedium of reading expressions such as 'his or hers' and 'he or she'.

CHAPTER ONE

Why You Cannot Afford to Neglect Training

THE SHROPSHIRE TRAINING & ENTERPRISE COUNCIL carried out a survey of the labour market in its area. The results, published in late 1990, included some fascinating (and horrifying) statistics.

The survey found that two thirds of employees in Shropshire had received no training at all in the previous *five years* and that 14 per cent of the companies surveyed had no training budget – which probably means no plans to train anyone.

The Shropshire TEC, looking ahead to the time when the 1990 recession is over and employers are looking for skilled staff, points out that they are unlikely to be available. Thirty per cent of the local unemployed were unskilled and had not had a job for over a year.

This means that would-be recruiters in Shropshire will have difficulty in recruiting trained staff when the time comes. They must therefore have a training scheme up and running to satisfy their manpower needs.

Obviously the company which has a training scheme will have the edge on those of its competitors who do not.

Not just in Shropshire

A report issued by the Road Transport Industry Training Board in the middle of 1990 also pointed to the need for training. About a third of the companies taking part in the survey had problems in finding suitable employees and more than three-quarters forecast that the problem would grow worse in the next three years.

Two quotations from the report are especially significant:

The road transport industry is beginning to suffer from shortages of skills in key occupational areas which, if unremedied, will create significant problems for the maintenance and repair of vehicles and the transport of goods and people.

and,

For many important skills there is a shortfall between the anticipated level of shortage and the number of employers who have adopted a training solution.

The latter statement suggests some boardroom heads firmly placed in the sand – or a cunningly hidden plan which will resolve the problem and enable their companies to stay in business.

Where the value lies

One of the difficulties in arguing the case for training lies in the fact that it is relatively easy to work out the costs but not so easy to determine the value received.

Let's consider a hypothetical situation but one to which we can all relate:

A shopkeeper takes on a young man (George) as a shop assistant. George has no previous experience of working in a shop or knowledge of the products sold in the shop.

George receives no training with the result that although not rude to customers he is not welcoming. No-one has made him aware of the simple courtesies (or the smile) which will encourage customers to buy from the shop.In addition George, having little technical knowledge of the products he is selling, cannot answer customers' questions about them. Nor can he advise the customers as to which products will best meet their needs.

The result? Customers will regard the shop as one in which the reception is unfriendly and the services unhelpful. They will take their business elsewhere. The lack of training will also have an adverse effect on George by damaging his confidence. Confidence is only one of a number of important benefits which training can provide.

The Benefits of training

Employee Confidence

An employee who, through lack of training, is lacking confidence is a sad and sorry sight. He will spend as much time worrying about what he is doing as he does doing it. He will probably take his worries home and spend sleepless nights. If you think this is an exaggeration try to remember how you felt if ever you have been in the position when you were not sure what to do or how to do it.

The lack of confidence does not only affect the employee. It damages the company.

The following are some real-life cases:

■ The insurance technician who had a backlog of paperwork which he was uncertain how to handle. Being afraid to ask his boss for help (a boss who needed training in management skills) he took some of the more difficult documents home and destroyed them. Eventually this was discovered and the man was sacked. The damage to the company was considerable – including the cost of recruiting a replacement

■ The young saleswoman who did not know enough about the product she was selling to sell it effectively. Her hesitancy and embarrassment when visiting customers reduced her credibility and that of her company.

After a number of customer complaints this saleswoman was given the training she needed and is now in charge of a substantial part of her company's sales operation. Before being given training she was close to being dismissed as someone unsuitable for the job

■ The man appointed to take over the management of a department – with no prior training in management skills. A superb technician, this man had been promoted simply because of his technical skills. He failed as a manager and ended up shunted sideways into a 'non-job', leaving an expensive mess and a demoralized department for his successor to sort out.

Finding himself unsure what to do when faced with disputes, organizational problems and similar management questions, this manager opted out. He sat in his office and occupied himself with the technical matters which he could handle confidently.

Planning and other management needs were neglected – as were his staff

It might be argued that all these people should have pointed out their own inadequacies and asked for training. This argument has some validity but it is management's role and responsibility to see that the situation does not arise in the first place.

When is confidence most vulnerable?
The person most likely to suffer from lack of confidence is the new employee. This is not normally the reason why companies have induction training schemes but they do have the effect of improving confidence.

Induction schemes are most frequently aimed at making the newcomer as productive as possible as soon as possible and this has a confidence spin-off.

There are, in addition, two other common situations in which training can be vital in ensuring that success is achieved:

■ When promotion of an individual is planned
■ When changes are to be made in systems, products, markets or any other significant company activity

Preparing for promotion
The failed manager mentioned earlier in this chapter illustrates the reason why training is needed when promotion is being planned.

However, the man concerned needed training to manage a particular department of a particular size doing a particular job.

There are many different situations involving promotion which require different and appropriate forms of management training. These range from section leading (say, two or three clerks) through charge hands, supervisors, foremen and so on up to board level. At each stage specific training is needed.

Without specific training the Peter Principle can come into play. This principle states that: 'In a hierarchy every employee tends to rise to his level of incompetence'.

While it is entertaining to poke fun at directors who have made it to the boardroom only to demonstrate that they are no longer able to do a good job, this phenomenon is not so funny when looked at from a profit angle.

The high-achieving manager who ends up as an incompetent director amounts to a costly burden which specific training might have prevented.

Training for confidence in the boardroom
According to a study carried out by Reading University (*Chief Executives as Crisis Managers*, published in 1990) British managers reckon that nearly half the problems faced by

businesses are caused by poor management. Sixty-three per cent of British companies thought that some kind of crisis was at some time inevitable and 89 per cent of American companies thought so.

Prevention of problems and the handling of crises is a number one requirement of board level executives – who should be the last people to create problems and crises.

How many of your directors have been trained in crisis management (e.g. a sudden and significant market change) or even in some of the associated subjects such as contingency planning?

Even more sad and sorry than the undertrained clerk is the undertrained and uncertain board of directors flailing around in the midst of a crisis.

Apportioning blame (a favourite occupation of the unskilled) and looking for excuses and scapegoats is no substitute for knowing what to do when the roof falls in or starts creaking.

When things change

'You'll soon get the hang of it' is one of the most over-used and abused statements heard in businesses which are introducing new technology. There is even a film on one-to-one training produced by Video Arts which uses those words as its title to illustrate how much more is needed.

Whenever a new system, product, computer or whatever is introduced employee confidence is on the firing line.

Training, that is real and substantial training, is essential before and during change. Without proper training staff will become worried and hesitant. Work will not get done and every foul-up will be blamed on 'this new machine' or other new system.

Alternatively the new technology – purchased at some expense – will perform badly or not at all.

The same principle applies when entering new markets

('How do I address a Saudi Prince?' asks the untrained salesman) or launching new products ('I'm not sure if this machine will work at low temperatures').

Employee productivity

It is self-evident that someone who has not been shown how to do a job will either not be able to do it or will make an attempt which is likely to result in mistakes. Despite this, people *are* thrown in at the deep end with inadequate or no training. The following are real-life comments made by junior employees in a medium sized British company:

- My training is inadequate and I make lots of mistakes. I have not been taught anything properly
- I cannot deal effectively with our customers because I have not had any training
- If I had had proper training it would have saved lots of wasted time. The thing is that I could have been more efficient
- All the juniors we took on last year have left. They had no proper training and yet were blamed for not getting the work done on time
- We should have finished all this work by the end of April. It is now nearly the end of June and we still have not finished it. The problem is that we have not had any real training so we waste time and make lots of mistakes

The managers responsible for the situation illustrated by these comments variously explained it away as follows:

- They ought to pick it up – I had to when I started
- We are all under a lot of pressure and we have no time to sit in classrooms
- We seem to be recruiting the wrong people

■ They have the manuals to refer to – why don't they use them?

These managers were stuck in a vicious spiral caused by ignorance and inability to get more work out of their people. Certainly the managers were under pressure – they spent much of their time sorting out the errors made by their own untrained people. Had some time been devoted to teaching the skills required, the managers would have had more productive time available for themselves. In addition their staff would have produced more.

The manager responsible for the young man who complained that he could not deal effectively with customers in turn complained that *he* had to spend time seeing the customers. Under pressure he admitted that the junior had not been trained to do the job and was blameless. The manager then complained about not having the time to train his junior. If only he had learned something about *how* to train people he would have known that with the right techniques the time problem can be beaten.

The human machine
Companies will service their motor vehicles and their machinery for the obvious reason that if they do not, the equipment will cease to work.

The human machine also needs servicing in a variety of ways in order to be able to work. One of the ways is training, without which people cannot even start to work effectively. Without on-going tuition they will not be able to do more or different work and they will develop the attitude that nobody cares anyway.

Everything else being equal, trained people produce more than untrained people. It's as simple as that.

Productivity starts from the top

The effect on juniors of managers with inadequate skills was amply illustrated by the comments of the juniors recorded earlier in this chapter. That this is by no means an isolated problem has been demonstrated by recent studies.

Professor Amin Rajan reports in *1992; A Zero Sum Game* that 'business success will only accrue to those companies with the technology, work skills and know-how to provide customized services and products'. Professor Rajan goes on to state that the losers will be companies without sufficient human expertise – in particular, management expertise.

This view was supported by Douglas Fraser, the Industrial Director of the National Economic Development Office at a conference in London in 1990. It was stated by Mr. Fraser that 'national under-performance can be put down to poorly educated management'.

Mr. Fraser added that 'a well-educated customer is more likely to be a demanding customer and a manager in a demanding environment is more likely to train his workforce'.

In other words if businesses are to succeed in a tough environment with demanding customers they must produce – and produce what the customer wants. This will depend at least in part on managerial know-how and the ability of managers to train their staff.

Avoid the one-off trap

Knowledge can quickly go out of date. The NEDC have reported that about half the knowledge acquired in obtaining a PhD in electronics will be out of date in only four to five years.

This principle applies to other skill areas and underlines the necessity for continuous training if ability to produce effectively is to be maintained.

Training someone once and assuming that this will last forever is a trap to avoid.

Employee Morale and Enthusiasm

Maintaining employee morale and enthusiasm at a high level is dependent on a number of factors, viz:

■ Making the employee feel valued
■ Providing scope for development
■ Providing challenge
■ Recognizing achievements

All these factors can, in part, be met by training.

Making the employee feel valued

Paying attention to someone makes them feel they are worth something to the company. If a manager discusses a junior's job with him, and especially if he asks for his opinions and ideas, it will motivate the junior. This is simple human nature at work.

Giving someone training has the same effect. The training (if properly sold to the employee) is a way of saying 'We think you are worth the investment of time and money'. In other words the employee will feel *valued* and will react accordingly.

Providing scope for development

People like to feel that they are getting somewhere and will become demoralized if that need is not met.

On the other hand they will feel more enthusiastic if the need is met.

Management's role is to provide scope for development by, for example, re-arranging work to use the skills of individuals to the maximum. Training plays a major part in this including:

■ On-job training
■ Off-job training
■ Controlled exposure to new experiences
■ Planning (with the employee) a step-by-step movement to

greater things as skills are acquired

Providing challenge

'Would you like to try your hand in export sales?' offers a challenge.

'Would you like to take a course in exporting and then take over export sales?' offers a challenge with a better chance of success.

It is the latter alternative which gets the best results and is seen by the employee as the best deal for him. This will motivate and probably improve productivity.

Recognizing achievements

Training can be a way for a company to say to an employee 'You have done very well Susan, and we think you are ready for greater things. We want you to take a management skills course'.

The fact of an employee receiving training is a public recognition of their potential and is equivalent to a public pat on the back. This also motivates.

Employee Loyalty

It is possible to buy – by means of a high wage or salary – the presence of someone in your company. It is not possible to buy his loyalty and commitment. Loyalty is obtained by other means and training is one of them.

Many companies experience a high turnover in staff who have been with them for only a few months. These people almost certainly joined their companies with high expectations and surveys have shown that it is failure to meet these expectations which causes early departures.

Training is one way to reduce the costly early resignation problem. A well-planned and executed induction programme followed by relevant skills training maintains the interest of an employee in the job and the company. Training implies a future, in addition to which the value of the knowledge gained is not lost on the ambitious worker.

Support for this view was aired at a national conference of the Institute of Personnel Management in 1990.

The chairman of the conference stated: 'They (young employees) want more and they want it now. They are rather assertive and if the organization doesn't offer them money, training and a career progression they aren't going to wait around passively and hope'.

Available employee skills

The wider the range of skills available to a company, the better placed it is to cope with problems and exploit opportunities.

In addition, if all managers at a particular level have had a basic training in skills not immediately related to their own job it is easier for them to work as a team with their colleagues.

One American company requires its employees to have undergone specific training in a range of business topics before promotion can be given. Thus a production supervisor will have had some basic training in say, Costing, Marketing, Contract Law and so on. Before being promoted to production manager level he would need further training in these subjects and possibly basic training in some others.

The result is that when, for example, a new product is being planned or launched, the production supervisor and all those involved will be able to understand the roles of their colleagues. The production manager will appreciate what the accountant is saying about marginal costing. The sales manager will understand the production manager's point about stock holding costs. The accountant will be aware of machine shop scheduling problems.

The result is a better effort from a united team who appreciate the needs of colleagues *and the firm as a whole*. Damaging parochial thinking goes out of the window.

At lower levels a wider range of skills means that employees can be switched from one area to another or can be used to cover a temporary absence.

All this makes a business more flexible, more effective and a more exciting place to work in.

These then are some of the values which training can provide. How does your company match up? How much are you missing out?

Try the following questionnaire. You need not show the results to anyone if you don't want to, so you can be brutally honest with your answers.

TRAINING NEEDS QUESTIONNAIRE

1. How often do you find staff are not taking action when they should due to lack of confidence or certainty?

Never ☐ Rarely ☐ Occasionally ☐ Frequently ☐

2. How often do you find yourself answering questions or otherwise sorting out problems which your subordinates should deal with?

Never ☐ Rarely ☐ Occasionally ☐ Frequently ☐

3. How often are employees promoted without prior training for the new job?

Never ☐ Rarely ☐ Occasionally ☐ Frequently ☐

4. How often do you have unreasonable (in your view) delays in the full implementation of new systems (e.g. computerization) and/or have persistent problems in the three months following implementation?

Never ☐ Rarely ☐ Occasionally ☐ Frequently ☐

5. How often do you have to clear up problems caused by 'clerical errors', failure to record a customer's telephone message correctly or other 'simple' matters?

Never ☐ Rarely ☐ Occasionally ☐ Frequently ☐

6. How often do you find yourself disappointed that a promising newcomer fails to maintain the standards of his first few months?

Never ☐ Rarely ☐ Occasionally ☐ Frequently ☐

7. How often do you find people from different parts of the company at odds with each other and that this, in your opinion, is due to lack of understanding of the other person's job?

Never ☐ Rarely ☐ Occasionally ☐ Frequently ☐

8. How often do you find yourself thinking that the people at the top are out of touch with reality and/or never seem to be able to make a decision – properly or at all?

Never ☐ Rarely ☐ Occasionally ☐ Frequently ☐

9. How often have you thought that you and the company would benefit if *you* could ever find the time for some specific training?

Never ☐ Rarely ☐ Occasionally ☐ Frequently ☐

How do you score?
First, any ticks in the 'Never' boxes should be re-thought because life is not like that. You may be right, but if so either you or your company are exceptional to say the least.

Having reconsidered your 'Never' score and adjusted it if necessary:

award 1 point to each 'Rarely' tick
2 points to each 'Occasionally' tick
3 points to each 'Frequently' tick

The worst score you can get is 27, which means you have some serious problems which training can help you to solve.

18–27 points suggests that your whole company set-up needs some close examination and that there is a lot that you can do which will improve profitability.

12–17 points suggests certain areas of activity could do with some attention and there is much to be gained.

6–11 points indicates a fairly high standard, with opportunities for improvement here and there.

0–5 points tells you to take a pat on the back or think again about how honestly you have answered the questions.

Of course not all of the inadequacies that you can see in your company can be solely attributed to lack of training. There may be other causes. However it is almost certain that appropriate and well-organized training can at least *contribute* to removing the problems. The rest of this book will tell you how to go about it.

SUMMARY OF KEY POINTS

1. Training can enhance the performance of your employees –
   and thereby the performance and profitability of your
   company by:
   - Improving employee confidence i.e. they will *know* what to
     do and how to do it
   - Raising productivity
   - Maintaining a high level of morale and enthusiasm
   - Stimulating loyalty to the company and reducing staff
     turnover
   - Providing a greater range and spread of skills resulting in a
     more flexible and capable organization

2. Training is needed throughout all levels of a business – for
   those on the way up and those at the top.

3. Change, e.g. introduction of new methods or products, is
   heavily dependent on sound training if it is to be successful.

4. People are like machines in that they need regular 'servicing'.
   Training provides the servicing.

5. Training is an on-going need and should not be treated as a
   one-off exercise to last for a life-time.

6. If you want to attract (and keep) good employees training is a
   'must'.

CHAPTER TWO

Planning Your Training for Profit

WHATEVER THE SIZE of your business you need a company plan of which your training plan will form a part. Your plan need not be complicated – indeed the simpler it is the more likely it will get you somewhere.

It should, whatever your size, be something more than a few jottings on the back of an old envelope but it need not be hundreds of pages of statistics and pompous statements. These huge and complicated 'corporate plans' so beloved of certain major organizations are largely ignored in practice and are often a waste of time.

Your plan will need to map out where you want to go and how to get there.

It will take into account:

- Your view of future customer wants
- Your products – and how they must be adapted to meet future customer wants
- Your finances
- Competition
- Your physical resources – machinery, vehicles etc
- Your human resources

The last of these is no less vital than any other aspect, and it can be argued that your people are your most important resource.

The finest product in the world and the most up-to-date and efficient machinery are all worthless if your people cannot sell the product and you lack the skills properly to operate the equipment.

It is on the skills of people that you will also depend for:

- Effective purchasing
- Sound production planning
- Efficient billing and other administrative systems
- High standards of customer service
- Control of costs
- Quality standards which meet the demands of the market

and above all, willingness and ability to overcome problems and take or create opportunities.

These skills are not inherited from birth and are unlikely to be gained by sitting next to Nellie or watching George for five years. They are most effectively learned (and most quickly) if formally taught. Management training is especially important as the born manager is a very rare bird. Most of those who think they are born managers are suffering from delusions.

Putting the people into a plan

Let us suppose that you have been jogging along quite nicely for three or four years with a couple of reasonably successful products. Profits have been satisfactory but not exciting.

You decide that it is important to raise profits and to introduce a new product.

You can see the day coming when one of your present products will begin to decline and this will make your business marginal or unprofitable. The new product should be available for sale in six months. You work out a plan of campaign including:

- Finalizing the design of your new product
- Developing new markets – particularly in France and Germany – with 1992 in mind

- Installing new production equipment
- Providing an after-sales service

You have the financial resources but what about the people? You must now ask questions about the skills needed in the future if the plan is to work:

- What new or additional production skills are needed?
- Do we have the language skills to sell effectively in France and Germany?
- Will we be able to handle export documentation, insurances and the like?
- What sort of people, with what technical knowledge, do we need to provide an effective after-sales service?

You will now look at the human resources you have got:

- Joe Fastlane, the sales manager, is a good German speaker but is 62 years old and retirement is in sight.
  He has substantial past experience of selling in Germany but not in France
- Bert Fiveiron, the deputy sales manager, is 40 years old and, you believe, a suitable successor for Fastlane. He has no experience of export sales and speaks no foreign languages
- The sales team have all been with you for some years and you have confidence in them. Their sales technique knowledge is good

You now devise a training plan for the sales side of the new product:

- Two of your more experienced salespeople will be made responsible for sales in Germany and France respectively and Fastlane will run a series of in-house teach-ins on exporting for them and Fiveiron

■ The two salesmen will also take 'total immersion' courses in German and French respectively
■ Fiveiron will take an external course in export procedures and documentation

This programme to be completed within three months.

During the next two months the two salespeople, assisted by Fastlane, will visit Germany and France to publicize the new product and negotiate with potential customers.

Fiveiron will teach the office staff the necessary export documentation and will sort out all the nuts and bolts of forms, records and computer procedures required.

In the final month before launch of the new product all concerned will assess progress and, as a team, plug any gaps or exploit opportunities to make the launch a greater success. One important aspect is to ensure that *all* the salespeople have a thorough understanding of the new product – its features and how these features translate into benefits for the customers.

Looking further ahead

A training plan will also be needed for Fiveiron to prepare him for taking over when Fastlane retires. In turn one of the salespeople will probably be selected to take the deputy sales manager job and will need training for this role.

Similar short and long term plans will be needed for employees concerned with production, after-sales service, distribution, administration and anyone else affected by the new product.

The essential requirements of a training plan

Most of the requirements are illustrated by the hypothetical example just described.

In summary:

- The plan must be designed to meet a perceived need based on forecasts of what is to happen. Training for the sake of it is likely to be a waste of money
- The training must be relevant and specific to individuals and the job they are to do
- A timetable must be included in the plan and progress against the timetable monitored by someone in authority. This is a particularly important provision as there is a marked tendency for things to give way in the face of urgent day-to-day demands
- Some contingency time should be built into the timetable to allow for sickness or other potential causes of delay
- Ideally more than one person will acquire essential skills to provide absence cover and back-up and to reduce vulnerability in case of a resignation or similar hiccup
- *The purpose of the training and its relevance should be explained to every person involved.* This will encourage commitment and remove the frequent comment: 'I don't know why I am on this training course'

These features should be included whether or not you are handling a specific project and ideally your overall company plan will include, amongst others, a *policy* for employee training.

This could be worded along the following lines:

Training Policy

The company recognizes the contribution that training can make to profits and competitiveness. The training needs of each employee will be reviewed each six months and a training plan maintained for each employee. A training budget will be set each 12 months.

On-going training – the questions to be asked

Once a year (or perhaps more frequently if things are rapidly changing in your industry) you must review your company plan. To identify the training necessary to carry out the company plan a series of questions should be asked:

- Are we planning any new initiatives which will require skills which we lack?
  e.g. New products
  New markets
  Acquisition of another business
  Meeting changes (e.g. 1992)
  Introducing computerization of production
- Are we, or will we be, dependent on one or two people for particular essential skills? If so, how vulnerable are we?
- Do we have enough trained people in the various parts of the business to enable us to expand? i.e. could progress be held back by lack of skills?
- Are there any aspects of our service to customers which have given rise to justified complaints and which indicate a need for improved skills?
- Do we have supervisory and management skills in sufficient depth to meet future needs?
- Which people will retire in the next 12 months and what skills will they take with them?
- What is our forecast of other forms of natural wastage? What must we do to replace skill losses?
- Are there any people whose full potential is not being developed? (i.e. we are not using all the talent available to us)
- Are there any areas of company activity which are weak (e.g. we have got it wrong too often)?

These, and possibly other questions peculiar to your business, will indicate areas where training could pay off.

The next step is to identify clearly which *individuals* should be trained and precisely how.

There must be a clear reason for every training course or session and this is best ensured by starting with a simple statement of what is to be achieved – an objective.

This objective can be expressed along the following lines:

Training Objective

'At the end of the training Jane Smith and John Brown will be able to:

(a)   Identify the data required for reliable sales forecasting
(b)   Use the XYZ computer system for analysing the data
(c)   Provide sales forecasts by product and geographical area.'

Such a statement avoids the dangers inherent in a 'general idea' such as to 'learn how to produce sales forecasts'. Some precision is required in order to identify clearly exactly what is to be learned (and what is not). This will help you to avoid the dangers of overlooking an essential aspect of the skills needed and paying good money for skills which are *not* required.

What the training plan will look like

Having done your 'training needs assessment' and made up your mind who needs what, the whole thing can be put together in a simple table which summarizes what you intend to do.

A table such as this will probably meet your needs:

TRAINING PLAN: JANUARY–JUNE 1991

Trainee	Subject or course	Reason	Completion date	Person responsible
Jones	Production planning	Need for more precision in production schedules	Feb 1st	Production manager
Smith	French	Expansion of export sales in France	March 30th	Export Sales Manager
Bloggs	Credit control	Setting up credit control department	Feb 28th	Accountant
Snooks	Centre lathe operating	Increase in machine shop capacity	April 10th	
Jackson	Centre lathe operating			Production manager

A copy of this plan provided to trainees and the people responsible – and to management in general – will ensure that everyone knows:

- Who is to be trained
- What they are to learn
- Why the training is required
- When the training should be completed
- Who is responsible for seeing it is done

The person responsible for seeing that the training is actually carried out is not necessarily the person (or organization) who will actually do the training. This will sometimes be the case – for example where on-job training is involved. It may also be the case that the trainee is being sent on an external course. Someone must be responsible for this and will have the following duties:

- To find – or assist in finding – the most appropriate course
- To arrange bookings on the course
- To brief the trainee fully on the reason for the training
- To de-brief the trainee on completion of the course and to report to management the outcome in terms of effectiveness

Not all courses will achieve their purpose and it is vital to spot this as soon as possible. The assumption must *not* be made that simply because young Jessie has spent a week at a computer training school she is now an expert programmer. Indeed, another role of the person responsible can be:

- To ensure that post-course practice takes place and to monitor results

Attention to this kind of detail can make all the difference between spending money and getting little for it and enjoying a good return on your investment.

For Pete's sake start at the top!

A common problem arises when a bright and enthusiastic junior is trained in a subject with which his boss is not familiar.

This can arise if, say, the distribution manager has learned his job over the years with no formal training. If his putative deputy is then sent on a distribution management course at a business college, the deputy may come back with all sorts of ideas of which the boss has no knowledge.

He might have learned:

■ Statistical techniques of varying kinds
■ Computer systems for vehicle scheduling and maintenance
■ Warehouse space allocation techniques
■ Visual stock-control methods

and so on.

The trainee may well come back to work fired with enthusiasm to use some of what he has learned, only to find that his boss neither understands them or has any intention of using them.

In a real-life case a deputy attended a management skills course. On his return his boss, having listened to some of the ideas in the deputy's mind said:

'That's all fine, you have done the bloody course now let's get back to work doing it my way'.

Not only is this a waste of money but it can have a devastating effect on the morale of the junior.

It is important therefore to start the process of bringing any new skills into the company at the level where working methods are decided. The boss must also be trained and convinced if his subordinates are to have any real chance of using what they have learned.

A note for recruiters

The principle of training first at the top can also apply when recruiting someone to bring new skills into your company. The newcomer can be blocked and frustrated by old hands who cannot or will not allow the newcomer to use his skills. This often results in the costly departure of the new recruit having once too often heard someone say 'That's not the way we do it' or 'We do things differently round here'.

Training the trainers

Your training plan may include an element – possibly a preponderance – of in-house training to be carried out by your own people. How well will they do it?

There are a few, a very few, individuals who can instinctively find effective ways to teach others. The vast majority of us will make a poor job of it without some training in how to train.

In-house instructors need to know:

- How to plan training sessions in a logical way
- How to encourage learning – and how to avoid the many things which will inhibit learning
- How to put it over in such a way that the trainee learns easily and quickly
- How to follow-up and reinforce the trainee's progress

Such skills can be taught quite quickly – a day with a professional trainer is normally enough. The difference between the work of the trained trainer and the guy who does it by the seat of his pants is normally very marked.

Who to train – a summary

The people to be trained include:

- Any in-house trainers (how to train)

- People who are expected to take on more responsibility e.g. promotion to fill a retirement vacancy
- Bosses whose subordinates are being taught skills which are new to the boss or the company
- People who are involved in a project or development which demands new or additional skills or knowledge
- People whose jobs will change as a result of new technology
- Those whose performance has been lacking or which must be enhanced to meet a more demanding market

What about some 'general' training?

Emphasis has been put on the importance of designing your training to suit the needs of individuals and the role they perform or will perform. This does not mean that a general training plan which covers groups of workers is out of place.

There are a number of areas where the group approach can pay off.

Basic Skills

A survey commissioned by the BBC, the Training Agency and the Adult Literacy and Basic Skills Unit revealed some worrying facts. The survey, carried out in Britain in 1990, showed that:

- More than one in ten people had difficulty calculating how much a dozen chocolate bars would cost and how much change they would get from £10
- Forty per cent could not divide a £30.35 restaurant bill among five people
- Forty-seven per cent could not work out 15 per cent VAT on £80
- Thirteen per cent were unable to add up £7.50, £2.00 and £15.00

Similar results were obtained in subtraction and multiplication, and twenty-nine per cent could not work out the area of a wall 12ft. × 8ft. Twenty per cent did not know what area meant!

Since these basic mathematical skills are required in a wide range of jobs it may pay you to run courses for any employees who are found to be lacking.

The same applies in written work skills. A leading company in the City of London runs letter-writing courses for all appropriate employees – including very senior ones and such professionals as barristers.

These courses deal not only with the structuring of letters but also in elementary knowledge such as:

- Correct use of apostrophes
- The correct plurals for words such as bureau
- The correct use of words such as data – e.g. avoiding its use as a singular: 'this data'
- When to sign off 'Yours sincerely' or 'Yours faithfully'

Such knowledge is by no means unimportant – especially if letters or other documents, in English, are being sent abroad to customers who may not be experts in English.

The City company referred to found a letter in which one of its executives had written:

'We will take statements from the deceased relatives'.

The absence of an apostrophe and an 's' added to 'deceased' made the writer and his company look more than a little silly – even though it was possible to work out what he was trying to say.

Computer skills
There is scarcely anywhere in industry and commerce where

computers have not made an impact.

Various surveys have shown that far too many people are lacking in computer literacy despite ever increasing dependency on computer systems.

It may pay you to train groups of people at all levels in at least the basics of computing. Managers in particular need to know more about the subject than can be picked up by reading the business press. If management lacks computer know-how it can find itself in the hands of its computer staff who can effectively control a whole range of company activities.

Conversely, if managers understand what, for example, a programmer has to do they will be more able to appreciate how long it takes to develop new systems and why. This was bought home to the director of a company who promised a major customer that it would be invoiced differently in future – and that each invoice would be backed up by an analysis of various costs.

Had he been able to appreciate what this would mean in terms of re-programming the sales ledger and invoicing system he might have at least consulted his computer staff before committing the company.

As it was he had to go back to the customer cap in hand to ask for time. Incidentally, the cost of making the changes ran into many thousands of pounds – and it was all changed back again a year later!

Business skills – for technical people

There are many technical people who have a limited knowledge of business in general or the company they work in in particular.

Computer specialists are perhaps the most obvious example and there have been many cases where the lack of non-computer knowledge has brought about disasters.

One medium-sized company started to train its computer team of four people in the business of the company and its objectives. All the trainees admitted that they had only a rough idea of what the company (in the financial sector) really did. None really understood the purpose of the facts and figures they were asked to produce, who the company's clients were and so on.

Not only did the training enable them to work more effectively with users (whose language they now better understood) but they were also able to suggest more efficient ways in which to meet their needs.

Other possible candidates for general training in business and the company's business are:

- Engineers
- Designers
- Accounting Staff
- Laboratory Technicians
- Typists
- Machine operators

All these are people who can be isolated from the mainstream of the business and be expected to do a job within limited boundaries.

An example of how training such people can improve profits can be found in a small company which trained its four secretaries in the basics of the business. Since the secretaries were frequently fielding telephone calls for absent executives the knowledge gained enabled them to deal with callers more effectively. In particular they were more frequently able to meet the callers' needs themselves rather than taking a message to be dealt with later when the executive returned. The beneficial effect on customer service and the image of the company was very marked.

The very top – training for the boardroom

There are companies which run induction courses for new recruits, management training for intended heads of department and organize specialist training for engineers, chemists, salespeople and so on.

How many of them train their directors? How many directors take their seat in the boardroom having had some formal preparation? The probable answer to both questions is very few.

Somehow we expect our directors to abandon their former departmental and divisional responsibilities and instinctively know what they should be doing as directors.

What directors should be doing

The directors' role should take into account the whole range of company activities and this means:

■ Having a sound understanding of all company activities and not just the narrow area from which they have come. Having been successively a salesperson, an area sales manager, sales manager and general manager sales does not equip someone to deal with problems of corporate planning, financial planning, diversification, long-range product development and so on. It is equally unlikely that any other route to the top will provide the skills needed effectively to handle such topics

■ Long-term thinking. The director needs to be able to recognize what needs to be done in anticipation of situations forecast for one or more years ahead. This in turn means:
 – taking a company-wide view
 – recognizing what is important as opposed to what is urgent
 – looking ahead to possible changes in the national and international industrial, financial and political scenery and

assessing the likely impact on the company
- Devoting time to thinking and discussion. One of the most difficult hurdles to overcome after the translation from line management to the board is that of sitting back and thinking. Having spent years of hands-on action dealing with problems and keeping things going it seems wrong to spend time in discussion and cogitation.

  The chances are that the new director will feel that he ought to be doing something. He will be tempted to continue doing what he did before and thus wreck the morale of his successor who wants to be left alone to get on with his new responsibilities

These boardroom skills can be taught – and much can be done before the director reaches the boardroom.

Some things positively not to do

The following misuses of training are all taken from real life and are positively damaging:

- *Making training a status symbol.* In some companies training is reserved for the favoured few – whether they need it or not. A few days away in a luxury hotel listening to a management guru expounding his latest theories may be a great ego trip for the VIPs. They can refer to it loftily at the bar of the golf club and trot out all the latest buzz-words to impress their friends. It will no doubt make them feel very important, but unless it has some relevance it is a waste of money. The fact that training is reserved for the VIPs will, in addition, be deeply resented at lower levels. They will come to regard training not as a valuable management tool but as a 'jolly' to be enjoyed when they finally make it to the executive offices. In other words training becomes equated with the reserved

parking space and the key to the executive wash-room.
- *Going overboard on training.* We can all become over-enthusiastic about a favoured 'management technique' or tool. Fans of management by objectives, discounted cash-flow and a whole range of operations research methods have come – and gone. Don't let your training get out of hand or it will fall into disrepute.

Such a mistake was made by a company which became so sold on training that it devised a points scheme for its staff. Everyone was expected to earn 50 points within a period of eight months.

Points could be gained by attending in-house courses (1 point) and a selection of external courses (5 points).

It was made clear to the employees that success in achieving 50 or more points would earn them favour, while failure would be damaging. The result was a frantic rush to get on courses – any courses – whether or not the training was of any value to the person concerned. To complicate matters the company offered points to anyone who ran a course (5 points) or made presentations to customers (5 points)!

Why giving presentations to customers was included is something of a mystery but it did have an effect on those with no opportunity to meet customers. It made them all the more eager to find places on courses – any old courses.

- There is no value in sending people on courses:
  - to give someone a change
  - without telling the trainee why
  - as a reward for good work
  - to get the trainee out of the office
  - because training is a 'Good Thing'
  - because someone had to go
  - to use up the training budget
  A company which sent a man on a training course to get

him out of the office did a remarkably good job of it *after* the course. They fired him on his first day back!

Another company sent a man on a training course only a month before he retired. When he protested, his boss said 'Don't argue about it: it is company policy that everyone must do this course'.

■ *Organizing in-house training out-of-hours.* There is an understandable temptation for a busy company to organize its in-house training in the evenings, lunch breaks or even at weekends.

This out-of-hours activity may be acceptable to directors and other senior executives – who have some choice in the matter – but it should not be imposed on juniors.

The junior and middle ranking employees of a company which arranged *voluntary* training sessions starting at the close of business expressed their views in these ways:

> 'Although attendance is supposed to be voluntary, anyone who does not turn up gets sarcastic comments from the heads of departments'.
> 'I want this training but after a day's work I am too tired to learn anything'.
> 'I have a long journey home and these sessions drag on. It makes too long a day'.

These and similar comments were made by almost everyone who was expected 'voluntarily' to attend the sessions and, perhaps worst of all, many employees felt a sense of guilt if they missed a session.

The fact is that if your people really need the training it is important. If it is important it should be a prime time activity. Tacking training on to the working day suggests that it is a second-class activity. It would not be surprising if the trainees took the same view.

SUMMARY OF KEY POINTS

1. Every company, large or small should have a training plan – which forms part of a company plan for the foreseeable future. The plans need not, perhaps should not, be complicated. The simpler the better.

2. The training needs of *individuals* must be identified in terms of what is expected of them now and in the future. Training for each individual should form part of a coherent plan for the team as a whole and plans for individuals should be complementary.

3. A sound training plan meets future demands of the company, is relevant and will be monitored. It should also be carefully and effectively communicated to all concerned.

4. A training policy should be worked out to ensure commitment – starting from the top.

5. Start your training scheme at the top by teaching the managers before you teach their subordinates.

6. Train your in-house trainers. There are very few born teachers.

7. Train also, people who are taking on more or new responsibilities – before they get them.

8. Consider your needs for some basic literacy and numeracy skills and how some more general training might improve your company's performance.

9. Some likely topics for your general training plan are:
■ Computer knowledge
■ Business skills – for technical people
■ Boardroom skills – for potential (or actual) directors

10. Avoid common mistakes such as making attendance on courses a status symbol rather than a response to a perceived need.

CHAPTER THREE

Training and Appraisal Schemes

Appraisal – a wasted opportunity?

ACCORDING TO A SURVEY of nearly 600 UK employers carried out in 1990 by *Personnel Today* and The Wyatt Company (*Performance Management 1990*) only about 20 per cent consider appraisal schemes to be effective.

This possibly means that around 80 per cent of UK companies are not getting much out of their appraisal schemes and there are of course, many companies with no scheme at all.

This information indicates the loss of a significant opportunity to improve employee and company performance. A properly conducted appraisal scheme can raise standards and cut costs and in some cases 'revolutionize' the business. There are advantages to be gained by the employee, his boss and the company – not least because appraisal is an excellent way to spot genuine trainee needs with great precision. Why then is there such a high level of failure to achieve any benefits?

The four causes of failure
Behind every unsatisfactory appraisal scheme are one or more of the following faults:

- The appraisers are not trained in how to use the scheme
- Appraisees are not sufficiently aware of what it is all for
- There is an absence of follow-up – which would normally involve some form of training
- The scheme is linked to salary increases

These problems will be dealt with later but it is first necessary to describe the appraisal process for the benefit of readers who are not familiar with it.

What is appraisal and what should it achieve?

The basic process is simple.

Each employee is interviewed once or twice a year at regular intervals by his boss.

The two people discuss the employee's performance, his problems, ambitions and general attitude to his work and the company.

In particular both people try to identify and agree the employee's strengths and weaknesses.

Having identified these problems, strengths and weaknesses a programme is agreed to exploit the strengths and eliminate or reduce the problems and weaknesses.

Both parties are likely to have some responsibility to carry out the improvement programme and the boss is responsible for seeing that it is done.

The achievements arising from the appraisal should be:

- A better understanding by boss and employee of obstacles to greater productivity and quality of work
- Removal of misunderstandings or gaps in knowledge in respect to company or departmental objectives and required standards of performance
- Awareness of factors which are inhibiting the performance of the employee – including how the boss manages his department, if this is a cause of difficulty
- Some positive action which can be taken to make the employee more effective

The last item on the list often involves training and can be expected to yield the most obvious pay-off – particularly because the training agreed on is likely to be highly relevant and clearly targeted.

How appraisal should be approached

There are a number of ground rules which must be adhered to if any real benefits are to be gained. The first of these govern the way in which the appraiser goes about his task and are related to the first of the faults already mentioned – the appraiser is untrained for the task.

Untrained appraisers tend to make the following mistakes:

Insufficient preparation
A minimum of essential preparation is required. The appraiser must:

- *Ensure that the employee is warned well in advance of his appraisal interview*, so that he has time to work out what he wishes to bring into the discussion. (N.B. Normally each appraisal interview will end up with the completion of a form. The form will include questions on performance, future action and so on. A blank copy should be given to the employee well before the interview to remind him of the type of things to be discussed.)
- *Ensure that the employee is aware of the nature of an appraisal interview*. In other words:
  - it is meant to be wholly constructive
  - it should be frank on both sides
  - it should be friendly and supportive
- *Book ample time in his diary for the interview*. An appraisal interview must never be rushed. Apart from the fact that someone's career is being assessed and affected the company has a vested interest in getting the best result from it. This will not be achieved in ten minutes. A full hour is more likely to be needed.

■ *Arrange a suitable place for the interview.* The environment should be 'neutral', for example a conference room. Ideally the two people will sit in comfortable chairs with *no desk between them.*

The presence of a desk (or even a table) is not only a physical barrier but a psychological one too. A desk adds a sense of formality and division which can result in appraiser and appraisee adopting an adversarial attitude. Such an attitude is unlikely to encourage valid or constructive results.

The venue should also be quiet. Telephone calls and other interruptions should be prevented. Any interruption will break the flow of constructive discussion, will irritate the appraisee and says to him 'This call (or whatever) is more important than you and your future'.

■ *Update his knowledge of the employee.* Lack of knowledge of what the employee does, how long he has been in the job and so on will make the appraiser's job next to impossible. It also has a devastating effect on the appraisee. In one such case the appraisee expressed himself as follows:

'He [the appraiser] had hardly ever spoken to me before. He had no idea of what my job involved and didn't seem to want to hear my version of it. As far as I am concerned it was a waste of time'.

Part of the problem in this case was caused by the appraisal being conducted by someone senior to the appraisee's boss. All appraisals require a close job relationship between the two people and normally the immediate boss should carry out the interview.

Even if someone very familiar with the employee and his work carries out the interview, it is highly desirable for the appraiser to read the employee's job description first. If no job description exists the appraisal may be a good opportunity to start preparing one – or to revise an out-of-date one.

Poor conduct of the interview

Appraisers must carry out interviews with sensitivity and care. In particular they should:

- *Start gently.* The appraisee may be nervous and still not sure of the true purpose of the discussion. He may be on the defensive and expecting to be subjected to a fault-finding interrogation.

  Such misunderstandings should be removed by a friendly re-statement of the purpose of the session. A few minutes' informal chat about some neutral subject can also help to settle the appraisee down and set the necessary relaxed tone.

- *Continue gently – and listen.* A common fault of untrained appraisers is to launch into a positive statement – which may be inaccurate – and then fail to listen to the response.

  Questions should be non-aggressive and non-accusatory. They should be designed to probe gently and to get the appraisee talking. By using the right questioning style the intelligent appraiser can uncover attitudes, aspirations, problems and opportunities which will not always emerge during the normal pressures of day-to-day work. Bosses who have conducted a successful interview have been known to express surprise, even astonishment, at what they have heard. The busier the boss the more unlikely he is to be aware of many of the things which are going on – despite the fact that most of us who manage people firmly believe that we do know what is going on.

- *Keep cool.* The appraiser must never allow himself to lose his self-control. Situations can arise where it is difficult for the two people to see eye to eye or find common ground. This can be exasperating and can result in harsh words. This kills any progress stone dead and is wholly counter-productive.

The golden rule for appraisers is constantly to try to see things from the appraisee's point of view.

■ *Be specific.* If there are any inadequacies in the appraisee's work they should: (a) be backed up by specific examples and (b) be described as opportunities for improvement and not put across as accusations or criticism.

General statements such as the following are of no help either in getting agreement or in identifying the training needed:

'Your relations with customers seem to be a bit "iffy".'
'You don't give me as much support as you could'.

Both of these remarks were used in real-life appraisals and, when pressed for an explanation of what was meant, the appraiser could offer no specific examples to support his case.

■ *Work towards agreement.* Both parties should look for areas of agreement and actively develop them. The appraiser must subtly control the interview to ensure that any point of agreement is recorded and built upon. It is often the case that once one or two relatively minor points are agreed the more significant items are dealt with more easily.

■ *Keep a written record of what is agreed.* The appraiser should write down – in front of the appraisee and visible to him – what is agreed. This ensures that nothing is overlooked when the form is completed at the end of the session. The appraiser must *not* write notes which the appraisee cannot see, as this will create suspicion in his mind and put him on the defensive.

■ *Sum up towards the end and confirm agreement.* All the notes should be jointly reviewed and the appraisee given every opportunity to express any change of mind. If the appraisee does change his mind it will no doubt be irritating to the appraiser but any irritation must be hidden. The appraisee's commitment to the results of the interview is vital and worth the time and patience required to get it. If necessary the items in question should be discussed again.

■ *Plan future action*. This is the pay-off part of the interview when *both parties* work out what needs to be done to remove weaknesses and exploit strengths.

The action plan might look like this:

JOHN SMITH : APPRAISAL JUNE 1991		
	SUBJECT	**ACTION**
1.	*Telephone Sales:* Enjoys the work and has achieved good level of success. Agreed could achieve better results after formal training.	Will attend external telephone technique course. To be completed by 1st September.
2.	*Correspondence with customer:* Letter-writing a weak area and finds difficulty in using dictation machine.	Will receive formal tuition in letter-writing from Sales Manager. Two half-hour sessions per week commencing 1st August. Will attend refresher course on dictation techniques on 23rd July.
3.	*Records:* Lack of easy access to sales and customer records i.e. wasting time and reducing efficiency.	To be given a computer terminal linked to central sales network. Keyboard skills training to be given by 2nd July and terminal to be made available by 3rd July.

It will be seen from this hypothetical example that the action plan can be made to address all the areas of improvement opportunity – including the provision of 'tools of the trade' which will make the employee more productive. Such opportunities, which do not always involve training, are frequently the result of appraisal sessions.

Some actual examples of opportunities are:

- The filing clerk who turned out to be a skilled word processing operator. No-one knew this before and there was a shortage of such people in the company!
- The part-time retired employee who had been a computer engineer. These skills were put to good use after the appraisal interview had revealed them
- The employee who jumped at an overseas posting which was difficult to fill. No-one had asked him before and he had not volunteered his interest. The discovery that he positively wanted the job saved taking on someone from outside the company

Don't imagine that valuable discoveries such as these only occur in big companies where people are less in the spotlight and lost in the crowd. They can also crop up in small companies – especially those where recruitment is very informal and the background of a recruit is not fully explored. Recruits will not always tell you everything that they have done before if it appears to be irrelevant to the job on offer.

What to do if agreement is not achieved

It is perhaps inevitable that from time to time agreement on some point or other is not possible.

The boss may believe that John Smith's work on the sales statistics leaves much to be desired whilst John himself reckons that he is doing a good job.

Normally such opposing views are caused by talking at cross purposes or a fear on the part of the appraisee of the consequences of admitting a weak aspect of his work. If patient discussion fails to resolve the problem it might be taken care of by the administration of your scheme. This should include provision for:

■ The form to be filled in jointly by the appraiser and the appraisee
■ Any area of disagreement to be highlighted. Some schemes allow for the appraisee to put his initials against conclusions or statements with which he agrees. The absence of an initial signifies his disagreement
■ Any area of disagreement to be reviewed by the appraisee and his appraiser's boss. In other words a form of appeal to a higher level

The mere existence of these provisions will discourage unreasonable attitudes on either side and will give the appraisee some reassurance that he will not be 'victimized' by a bad manager.

The final requirement – follow-up

The most successful appraisal interview and the best of resulting plans will all be wasted if there is no follow-up.

Someone, normally the boss who carries out the appraisal, should see that the plan of action agreed is in fact carried out.

Any external training courses must be found and booked. Internal training needs organizing and those involved must be thoroughly briefed on what is required and why.

Monitor the results

Some provision must be made to monitor results to see that the required skills are being taught and learned. In some cases the trainee himself may be responsible for various arrangements – such as enrolling in an evening class. The follow-up should extend into the quantity and quality of the trainee's work.

Improvements in the trainee's contribution to the company will have been one of the primary reasons for the appraisal and the proof of the pudding will be in the eating. There may have been some mis-judgement as to what training was required or its duration. Alternatively some aspect may have been overlooked. At all events remedial action may be required.

Linking appraisal with salary awards

If an employee's weak points are to be dealt with it is obvious that they must be openly identified. This is one of the purposes of the appraisal interview.

It should also be obvious that no normal human being will readily admit his weaknesses if by doing so he jeopardizes his chances of a salary increase.

The use of appraisal schemes as a means to assess salary worth is widespread and misses the point that appraisal is a basis for the future and not a means to calculate reward for the past. Salary awards should take into account a range of factors not all of which can be influenced by either the appraisee or his boss, and individual performance is not likely to determine the outcome. Factors which may influence salary levels include:

- Job grading
- Market rates for the job
- Agreements with unions
- Age and length of service
- Future potential
- Formal qualifications

There is no reason why an employee should not be told what has influenced his salary award – including his own performance – but this should be kept entirely separate from his appraisal.

Is there anything else that needs to be done?

There are three other steps you can take to make your appraisal scheme more effective:

■ *Make provision for the biter to be bit.* Effective appraisal interviewing should be part of every manager's range of skills. Managers should also be dedicated enough to pay attention to the follow-up stage to make sure something useful actually happens. These skills can be monitored in turn by the appraising manager's own boss when the appraiser is himself appraised.

A poor performance as an appraiser should be spotted and the necessary steps taken to rectify it. The knowledge that this will take place will encourage appraisers to do a good job of it.

■ *Keep the employee involved.* Apart from any training which does take place the employee needs to be psychologically involved. One way to do this is to ensure that he is provided with a copy of the completed appraisal form.

One company would not do this on the grounds that the appraisal results were confidential! In other words the employees were effectively told that the jointly-agreed conclusions of a discussion in which they took an equal part were not for their eyes. The only conclusion which the employees could reach was that either the whole thing was a nonsense or that something nasty was added to the form later. Appraisal interviews in the company concerned yielded little action of any value.

The possession of the form – which will contain the plan of action agreed – can be used by the employee to:
  – Check that what was agreed is being carried out
  – Remind him of anything he has to do himself
  – Read prior to his next appraisal. Last year's plan can often be a good starting point for this year's discussion

■ *Appraise regularly and on time.* The manager who says that he is too busy to hold his appraisal interviews and postpones them is saying to the employee – 'The files on my desk are more important than you, your work and your future'.

Postponed interviews tend to disappear altogether and, if

this practice spreads, the whole scheme disappears. This has happened more than a few times and the root cause is often the same. The appraisers have not been adequately trained – or trained at all – and find the interviews difficult. The result is a 'too busy' excuse.

The future of the company, which is influenced heavily by the future performance of the employees, is too important to be treated in this way. The files on the desk may be genuine and *urgent* but the appraisals are *important*.

What should your appraisal form look like?

Let's start with what it should *not* look like. It should not be complicated and try to cover every aspect of every job in the company. The form which tries to do this will be confusing and largely irrelevant to any particular employee.

It should avoid giving scores (e.g. points out of ten) for such things as:

- Punctuality
- Personal appearance
- Decorum

Nor should it be full of headings which are difficult to interpret or be objective about such as:

- Dedication
- Timeliness
- Commitment
- Co-operation
- Attitude

One form in use by a major company asked for a judgement on the employee's 'ability to concentrate' – a cause of much fruitless debate.

None of these things have any place in a forward-looking

scheme. The essential requirements are covered by a form along these lines:

APPRAISAL INTERVIEW SUMMARY

NAME:	JOB TITLE:	DEPT:
APPRAISED BY:	DATE:	
Agreed obstacles and difficulties	Action to be taken	
Agreed areas of opportunity	Action to be taken	

ADDITIONAL APPRAISEE'S COMMENTS:

ADDITIONAL APPRAISER'S COMMENTS:

A non-restrictive form such as this offers the flexibility for both parties to seek the things which really matter and come up with something imaginative.

Under 'obstacles and difficulties' any notes on weaknesses can be included. Strengths to be exploited can appear under 'areas of opportunity'.

A summary in a few lines

Successful appraisal with profitable results will be achieved when:

- The emphasis is on looking forward
- Criticism is excluded and replaced by goal-setting
- Discussion is based on specifics and not generalities
- Goals are specified, precise and generally agreed
- Action is specific and monitored
- Appraisers are helpful, willing to listen and try to see things from the employee's point of view

The result should be some truly relevant training plans, tailored to the individual and cost-effective.

How good is your appraisal scheme?

You may have an uncomfortable feeling that your appraisal scheme is not getting you anywhere. You may feel that it:

- It is all a bureaucratic nonsense
- It achieves little or nothing
- It is tolerated rather than enthusiastically supported
- It takes up too much time
- It makes no discernable difference to company performance

If you have some or all of these feelings the cause of the problem probably lies in the way in which your scheme is carried out. Try this test:

APPRAISAL EFFECTIVENESS TEST

Have your appraisers been formally trained?   YES ☐ NO ☐

Are your employees fully aware of the purpose
of appraisal?   YES ☐ NO ☐

Do realistic plans result from appraisals?   YES ☐ NO ☐

Are appraisees fully involved in designing the
training plans?   YES ☐ NO ☐

Is the implementation of training plans fully
monitored?   YES ☐ NO ☐

Is there any arrangement for evaluating the
results of any training?   YES ☐ NO ☐

Do your appraisers, without fail, carry out
appraisals on the agreed date?   YES ☐ NO ☐

Are appraisals *always* carried out by someone
with first hand knowledge of the employee
and his work?   YES ☐ NO ☐

Is your appraisal scheme entirely distinct from
salary award procedures?   YES ☐ NO ☐

How did you score? A series of 'Nos' is bad news. One or
two indicate serious flaws in your scheme and the aspects
concerned need looking into.

You may of course have no appraisal scheme in your
company and you are wondering if there should be one.

TRY THIS SELF TEST

Have there been times in the past when I have struggled to do a job as a result of lack of training?   YES ☐ NO ☐

Have I ever felt or do I feel now that my boss does not fully understand the problems that I face?   YES ☐ NO ☐

Do I see colleagues struggling to cope?   YES ☐ NO ☐

Do I have subordinates who lack skills?   YES ☐ NO ☐

Has the company ever failed to prepare me by training for promotion or new work?   YES ☐ NO ☐

Have I strengths which the company does not recognize or use?   YES ☐ NO ☐

Have I ever thought that the talents of colleagues are wasted?   YES ☐ NO ☐

Does the company fail to recognize potential and lose good people as a result?   YES ☐ NO ☐

'Yes' answers to these questions indicate opportunities for performance and profit improvement by using appraisal to spot training needs.

A thought for chief executives

Are you the chief executive? If so, try the self-test in these ways:

■ Take yourself back to, say, five years before you became chief executive and answer the questions on the basis of your memory of how you felt then. Now ask – 'Has the company changed anything since?'
■ Persuade three people from different levels in the company to answer the questions. (You will have to find people who

will give you truthful answers – not what they think you would like to hear). You will also have to assure them that there will be no unpleasant come-back to answers which are not favourable to your company

This mini-research exercise could point the way to some very useful action on your part.

SUMMARY OF KEY POINTS

1. An appraisal scheme is a first class way to identify training needs. The precision with which this can be done will result in economic use of your training budget and will ensure that training hits the right targets.

2. Three basic errors must be avoided:
   - Failure to train the appraisers
   - Poor explanations to appraisees
   - Linking the appraisals to salary awards

3. To be successful appraisal interviews must be well prepared, sensitively handled, constructive, forward looking and result in an action plan.

4. Action plans must be followed up.

5. An 'appeals procedure' is needed if there is failure to agree.

6. Keep your appraisal form simple and do not allow it to inhibit flexibility. Appraisal should not be a bureaucratic exercise.

7. Complete the questionnaires and take action to set up an appraisal scheme or sort out the shortcomings in an existing scheme.

CHAPTER FOUR

Training and Delegation

What is delegation?

ACCORDING TO A TRAINING COURSE handout provided by the Industrial Society delegation is:

> the practice of giving a subordinate the necessary authority to make decisions in a specified area of your work or function. You retain accountability.

This is probably as good a definition as anyone has devised without taking another hundred words or so to do it. However, the definition should be wider in order to take account of some very important points viz:

- The subordinate must be willing to take on the work involved
- The subordinate must be capable of doing the work – which may mean training before the work is handed over
- The work involved may not be limited to decision-taking – some routine activities may be involved

If the first two of these points, namely willingness and capability, are not met then handing over the work is *not* delegation. It is DUMPING – an activity often confused with delegation and frequently damaging to all concerned.

Dumping is used by unprofessional managers to get rid of work they find irksome, with no consideration for the unwilling subordinate or how it may affect the company. The ill-effects of dumping are then sometimes used as an excuse for not delegating by inadequate managers who are afraid to delegate.

True delegation is a valuable technique of management which benefits all concerned –

The benefits of delegation – to the boss

- A reduced workload resulting in more time for the management functions of planning, organizing and looking for opportunities
- Greater use of the human resources available and hence more production for the same budget
- Development of skills among subordinates which will result in a more effective team

The last two of these benefits will result in a better departmental performance which will enhance the boss's reputation.

Do you need to delegate?

You may have something to gain which is more specific than the benefits just listed. To spot it try this questionnaire which will tell you whether or not you are delegating enough and can guide you to personal advantages:

DELEGATION NEEDS TEST	
Is there any work which you do which could be done by your subordinates?	YES ☐ NO ☐
Do you put in more working hours than your subordinates?	YES ☐ NO ☐
Do you fail to meet deadlines from time to time?	YES ☐ NO ☐

Do you find yourself with too little time for management activities?	YES ☐ NO ☐
Do you involve yourself in detail because you prefer it or you feel safer?	YES ☐ NO ☐
Are you frequently having to spend time with subordinates making decisions and giving advice?	YES ☐ NO ☐
Do you take work home at nights and on weekends?	YES ☐ NO ☐
Do you find you have insufficient time for general conversation with your subordinates?	YES ☐ NO ☐
Do you keep a close eye on the details of your subordinates' work?	YES ☐ NO ☐
Do you feel that if you are not continually under pressure that you are not doing your job or earning your pay?	YES ☐ NO ☐

How do you score? Ten ticks in the NO column means that you have no delegation problem. Ten ticks in the YES column means that you are not only facing a serious problem but probably a heart attack or nervous breakdown as well.

You may be one of the managers who finds it hard to delegate for one or more of 'the classic reasons'.

The 'classic reasons' for non-delegation
1. *'My staff are already overloaded.'*

This *may* be true but there are many managers who are mistaken about it. Parkinson's Law (that work expands to fill the time available) is frequently in play in departments with a non-delegating manager. The manager sits in his office overloaded with files and work while his staff, with not enough to do and feeling guilty about it, spread their work out. The poor devils have to *pretend* to be busy even to the extent of going home late each night. This is what the boss does so they feel that they must do it too. The author has seen this situation many times and when the staff are asked if they would like work to be delegated to them they jump at it.

So, ask your people. Don't assume that there will be a department full of camels with broken backs.

2. *'My staff are not skilled enough to do the work.'*
Really? Is that because they have not been trained? The solution is obviously in the hands of the boss who can resolve the problem by organizing some training.

The 'classic reasons' are often a smokescreen hiding some ill-founded fears and the real, unspoken, objection to delegation.

The real reasons
1. *'If I delegate to my people one or more of them may do so well that he will be seen to be better than me. If so, he could replace me.'*
The other side of the coin is that if there is someone identified as the boss's successor who can take his job then the boss is available for promotion. Promotion is often not given because there is no-one believed to be good enough to replace the person under consideration.

2. *'If I give work to my subordinates someone may think that I am not able to do it myself.'*
No one ever got anywhere by overwork and it is no shame to take help from juniors. That is one of the reasons that managers have staff working for them.

The benefits of delegation – to the subordinate

The benefits to the person on the receiving end of delegation are potentially substantial but often overlooked. However, these benefits will only be gained by effective and *well-conducted* delegation (about which more later). They include:

- *Improved morale and motivation.* Delegation says to the subordinate:
  - I have confidence in you
  - I respect your abilities
  - You are ready for better things
  - I want you to progress

  In other words it is a public recognition of the person and, as with any form of recognition, is a great motivator. (Dumping of course is likely to de-motivate.)
- *Enhanced sense of status.* It is not always necessary to give someone a new or more fancy title to indicate his status. The responsibility for new, more important work also adds something to status. This is pleasing to the recipient and is another way to motivate.
- *Greater 'market value'.* The successful taking over of new, higher level work – or additional work – enhances the employee's value to the company. This should eventually be reflected in the employee's wage or salary.
- *Improved job interest.* A change is as good as a rest and new work breaks the old routine and gets the brain working. The more variation in the work and the more room for decision-taking there is the more interesting and exciting it becomes.
- *Challenge.* This is an overworked word and is sometimes used to con a junior into accepting some dumped work. The challenge must be real – as it will be if the delegation is genuine.

  All the behavioural science gurus who have studied what makes people tick at work list challenge as one of the factors. Hertzberg, Maslow, McGregor and Likert for example point out, in various ways, how people are stimulated by *opportunity* for achievement. Giving them something new can present them with an opportunity.

The benefits to the subordinate will rebound to the advantage of the boss and the company. A well-motivated team whose members feel that they have a worthwhile job to do will work better and perform in a way which reflects credit on the manager. The converse is also true. As one disgruntled employee put it: 'This department is a boring place to work in. He [the manager] hogs all the interesting work for himself. We get all the routine stuff and we have no chance to shine or learn anything'.

The message to managers is obvious!

Hopefully, the benefits of delegation are clear. The next step is to consider how it should be done. The doing involves training and brings us to the essential link between delegation and training.

How to go about it

The first step is for the manager to look at his own work and divide it into two main categories, viz:

- Work which I need not do myself
- Work which I *must* do myself e.g. confidential or security matters

Listing all the work done is not always as easy as it might seem, and identifying everything (including all the odds and ends) can take some time. One way to do it which will ensure that nothing is left out is to keep a work log for a week or two. You may be familiar with this if you have studied time-management and heeded the advice that keeping a work log shows up any wasted time. It will also reveal work which you do which you will realize you need not do once you have seriously thought about it.

A simple form is required such as this:

WORK LOG		DATE:
TIME	**WORK DONE**	**COMMENTS**
8.00 – 8.30		
8.30 – 9.00		
9.00 – 9.30		
9.30 – 10.00		
10.00 – 10.30		
10.30 – 11.00		
11.00 – 11.30		
11.30 – 12.00		
12.00 – 12.30		
12.30 – 1.00		
1.00 – 1.30		
1.30 – 2.00		
2.00 – 2.30		
2.30 – 3.00		
3.00 – 3.30		
3.30 – 4.00		
4.00 – 4.30		
4.30 – 5.00		
5.00 – 5.30		
5.30 – 6.00		
6.00 – 6.30		
6.30 – 7.00		

Using the form

Using any terms which suit you, fill in the 'time' and 'work done' columns as you go through the day.

Don't leave something out because it is relatively unimportant or takes only a few minutes. These bits and pieces add up and you may be surprised how much they add up to.

And don't tell yourself any lies about what you are doing.

This check on how you spend your time need only be seen by you and it will pay you to be brutally honest.

At the end of the day look back at what you have done and jot down some reactions in the comments column.

The result might look something like this:

WORK LOG		DATE:
TIME	**WORK DONE**	**COMMENTS**
8.00 – 8.30	Checking mail	Could secretary do this?
8.30 – 9.00	Dictating – using machine	Half of work was routine
9.00 – 9.30	Checking Blogg's figures	No errors found – was it necessary?
9.30 – 10.00 10.00 – 10.30	Attending office admin. meeting	Nothing important discussed – could send delegate in future?
10.30 – 11.00	Analysis of sales figures	Could Smith do this in future?
11.00 – 11.30	Financial planning meeting	Should have been better prepared
11.30 – 12.00	" "	

These entries – imaginary but based on actual experience – suggest:

■ Checking the mail could be done by a secretary or someone else. If someone is trained to pick out the items requiring the manager's attention he could leave the rest to someone else. The secretary, for example, could compose acknowledgement letters and the like and deal with other routines

- Was it really necessary to check Blogg's figures? Responsibility could be delegated to Blogg (which will probably please him) and, if there is any good reason for it, a spot check could replace a regular check
- The office administration meeting is one which could be attended by a subordinate – perhaps giving him valuable experience of involvement in meetings
- Analysis of the sales figures is another routine which is probably nothing more than the use of some simple arithmetic. The result may be important but someone else could be taught the analysis
- Lack of preparation for the Financial Planning meeting could be serious. If all or much of the preceding work had been delegated there would have been time for more preparation

Looking at your work like this will enable you to identify your delegation opportunities and also begin to spot the people to whom you might delegate and what training they may need.

In summary what this stage accomplishes is a set of answers to the questions:

- What work do I do now?
- Why am I doing it?
- Is there any real reason why I must keep doing it?

The next step is to answer two more questions:

- Is there anyone who could take over some of this work?
- What training will I have to arrange?

Match them up
Prepare a list of all the jobs you feel that you can delegate. Then

prepare a list of the people to whom you might delegate. Now match jobs with people.

It will then be necessary to discuss the intended delegation with the people concerned and to identify *with their participation* the training they will need.

You may find that there will be some resistance from one or two people – despite the benefits of the delegation to them.

There are a number of potential reasons for this which you must deal with:

- *Fear that they will not be able to cope.* You must offer reassurance that they will be properly prepared by training and that you have complete confidence in them.
- *Fear that they will make mistakes and get in trouble as a result.* Further reassurance must be given that it is inevitable that mistakes will be made, that this is expected and that support not complaint will be the result.

Having agreed the work to be delegated with the people a number of other aspects must be cleared up before training commences:

- Any additional authority must be agreed
- Any additional resources (e.g. a computer terminal) must be agreed
- All the people connected with the individual or the department must be advised so that no-one has any doubt as to who will being doing what in future.

Now prepare the programme and implement

A timetable of instruction can now be drawn up and training can start.

As soon as enough training has been completed – perhaps covering *part* of the work to be handed over – the subordinate can start to practise the new work.

If the training is likely to be lengthy and if the job can be conveniently divided into a number of parts, it is often advantageous to tackle the work in sections. The advantages are that:

■ The trainee has less to learn at a time – making the learning easier
■ The manager has a reduced problem of finding time to teach
■ Actually doing the job – even if only part of it – at an early stage means that the benefits of the delegation are enjoyed earlier

Check progress – sensitively.

As the learning and practice go along the manager and subordinate must review progress together. Any difficulties must be patiently sorted out before moving on to another stage and, if necessary, reassurance given to the subordinate.

Two golden rules should be observed:

■ *Any spot checks should be made with the knowledge of the subordinate.* Do *not* take a clandestine look at the work being done after the subordinate has gone home. Any subsequent comment you may make will suggest that you don't trust your subordinate and that you are spying on him. This will kill his enthusiasm (and trust in you) stone dead.
■ *Give the subordinate a chance to get on with it.* The boss who fusses about asking questions and interfering every five minutes makes his subordinate very fed up. Constant enquiries – 'You have checked the prices haven't you?', 'You won't forget to send a copy to production?', 'Have you done such and such?' – are thoroughly irritating and will demoralize the subordinate.

The link between delegation and appraisal
It will be seen that both appraisal and the analysis which leads

up to delegation can identify training needs with some precision. The appraisal interview can also reveal opportunities for delegation. The appraisee may well reveal his aspirations and, if so, these should be looked upon as an opportunity to be exploited to everyone's advantage. The results of a delegation programme can be discussed during the next appraisal – giving both parties a formal opportunity to review progress and look for other useful developments. A calm, considered review is rather less likely during the rush and tear of everyday activity.

Some more dos and don'ts of delegation

- Don't say, 'I can do the work quicker myself'. Of course you can. So could the guy who first delegated the work to you
- Don't say, 'I have no time to delegate'. You must *make* the time or end up doing all the work yourself – probably in a state of exhaustion. Failure to find the time only makes the situation worse and your own work quality will suffer
- Don't say, 'I have no suitable staff'. Your staff, their skills and what they do all day are *your* responsibility. Train them to make them suitable
- Do remember that delegation, like every other aspect of business, involves risks. Do allow for mistakes to be made – minimizing them with careful training and support
- Do give praise when the subordinate has earned it
- Be prepared for the subordinate who, rather than seriously trying to do the delegated work, finds it easier to keep going back to the boss for help. While some sympathy is needed for people with difficulties, draw the line when you feel that someone is not really trying

SUMMARY OF KEY POINTS

1. Delegation frequently requires training of the person to whom work is to be delegated – neglect of the training is a common cause of failure.

2. There are benefits to the boss, the subordinate and the company when delegation is properly handled.

3. Some bosses fail to realize that they need to delegate – some are afraid to delegate.
     A self-test may make you think.

4. There are some 'classic reasons' for non-delegation. These do not stand up to close scrutiny.

5. Delegation must not be confused with 'dumping'. A process should be followed which will lead to the delegation of the right things to the right people in the right way.

6. A work-log can point to work which can be delegated.

7. Work to a programme of delegation (which will include any necessary training) and avoid the common mistake of interfering and 'spying' on the subordinate.

8. Take advantage of the link between appraisal and delegation. Both will help to make your training profitable.

CHAPTER FIVE

Do-It-Yourself Training

The advantages of DIY training

THERE ARE SOME definite advantages in doing your own training – as opposed to sending people on courses. The advantages are:

- Potentially lower costs
- You control what is being taught and learned
- The training can be closely geared to your company situation, products etc.
- Trainers will be better aware of the environment in which the trainees work, their individual needs and problems
- Trainers will have a vested interest in seeing that there are useful results from the training – the trainers will have to live with the results of their work

However, training is not so easy as some people think. It is not simply a case of picking someone with the required knowledge and pitching him into a classroom with a bunch of trainees.

Teaching is a skill which must itself be learned.

Training your trainers

Paradoxically, unless you have a suitably experienced person on your staff, do-it-yourself training must start with some outside help. Your trainers must be trained. This can be done by sending them on an appropriate course but may be better done by employing a specialist consultant to do the job on your premises. The advantages of the latter option are:

■ The *nature* of the training that is needed can be assessed and a programme to suit *your* company can be devised
■ The *level* of training can be geared to suit your people and situation
■ Any particular and unusual requirements can be identified and catered for

The disadvantage is that the cost may be higher than sending one or two people on an external course. However the cost could be lower if several trainers are to be trained while a higher cost could be justified if the result of the consultant's work is more effective. The requirement is to obtain some quotations and exercise your judgement.

You may have some people who need little in the way of formal teaching to make them into effective trainers – for example people who are experienced in making sales presentations. For such people the following notes may give them enough to get started:

What trainers must remember

There are some undeniable characteristics of good (and bad) training which, if the trainer uses (or avoids) will go a long way to making the training sessions pay off.

Plan it carefully

Training sessions require a lot of thinking about. The first step is to consider – and discuss with the trainees – exactly what it is they need:

■ How basic should the training be?
■ What do the trainees know already?

■ Which aspects are likely to be the most difficult to learn?

and, most important of all:

■ What is the objective to be achieved by the training?

Remember, the objective should be expressed in precise terms of what the trainees will be able to do when the training, including any supervised practice, is completed.

Next, consider what material and facilities will be required. Will you need:

■ Examples of forms and other documents?
■ Machinery or computer equipment?
■ Handout notes and checklists?

You will almost certainly gain from using visual aids. It is one thing to describe something and quite another to demonstrate it or show a picture of it. You can consider:

■ Flip charts: a cheap and easy way to illustrate your point
■ Overhead projector: using prepared slides or making them up as you go along
■ Slide projector: a little more expensive but often worth it
■ Videos: these can be hired, purchased or, at some expense, made for you. (Some notes on how to go about having a video made for you are provided in Appendix I)

Role-play may be another form of 'visual aid'. This is especially useful when training in subjects such as negotiation technique. Thirty people who took part in negotiation technique courses all stated that the role-playing was the most valuable part. The role-play enabled them to practice, in simulated real-life situations, the concepts, tactics and techniques that they had learned. Not only did they confirm that what they had been taught actually worked, but the role-play also helped to fix in their minds the ideas put to them.

Where forms and the like are being used try to take completed ones from real life. They should be representative of what normally happens but, if there is an occasional departure from the norm, you might illustrate that too with an example.

Any machinery or other 'tools' should be in good working order and typical of what would normally be used in the job concerned.

Sorting out the detail

By this stage you will have decided broadly what is to be taught and the materials you will use. Now the training sessions can be designed in more detail. The following steps should be taken:

■ *Decide what is the most logical sequence.* What should come first? What must be taught to make subsequent sessions comprehensible?

It is only too easy to get things in the wrong order or to leave something out altogether. Trainers are usually so familiar with the subject that they regard some information as 'obvious'. Never do this. *Always look at it from the trainee's point of view.* What is obvious to the trainer may well not be obvious to the trainee.

One well-meaning trainer spent an hour teaching a group the statistical technique of 'standard deviation'. They were taken through the mechanical process of working out standard deviation figures and then asked to suggest ways in which the technique might be applied. None of the trainees could offer any answer because, as one trainee put it, 'You have not told us what it means. We can work out the number but what does it tell us?' The meaning of the figure was so well known to the trainer that it had not occurred to him that the trainees would be baffled by it. He should have started the session with an explanation of the concept

■ *Decide what part of the training can best be dealt with by the use of visual aids, a demonstration or perhaps role-play.* A discussion session may also be useful to put something across more vividly and to imprint it on the trainees' minds. The visual aids or briefings for role-play must be prepared and checked to see that they are complete

■ *Work out the training.* Short sessions are more effective than long ones and if at all possible give the trainees a break after 40 minutes. This is the maximum that most people can tolerate before fatigue and boredom begin to take effect.

Breaks need not involve bed rest or a visit to the local pub. A change of topic, method or pace will do. The following can be built into the programme, in addition to normal tea and meal breaks:

- discussions
- films
- demonstrations

or two minutes' walk around the block to stretch the legs and clear the mind

■ *Choose the place.* Training sometimes has to take place at a work site such as the machine shop of a noisy factory. There is nothing wrong in this providing the opportunity is given to review and discuss what has been learned in a quieter environment.

Ideally, training will take place in a pleasant and quiet environment – away from distractions such as telephones and people coming and going.

There should be ample space and an easy line of sight to flip charts, blackboards or screens.

You may decide to hold your training sessions in an hotel or conference centre. Some of the points you should watch out for when selecting the venue are described in Appendix III

■ *Choose your groups.* Try as far as possible to select people to be trained together who have a similar level of knowledge and experience. An experienced trainer can often find ways to deal with the problems of a mixed-skill group but it is not always easy. It is better, by careful selection, to avoid such problems as having the whole group held back by one or two less knowledgeable people who find the going harder.

Sometimes, however, it is a useful technique deliberately to include one or two more experienced people in the group who can raise standards and help the others. This is especially applicable where the trainees will be working in syndicates on problems or projects

■ *Communicate carefully.* All trainees must be given adequate notice of the course they will attend and – especially important – why they are listed for it. Avoid communicating this information by memo alone. A brief personal chat with each trainee sets a more friendly tone and gives them the chance to ask questions.

The objective and the benefits of the training to the individuals should be clearly explained. If the trainees can see some positive personal advantage in the training they will be better motivated to learn. It must not be assumed that they will work this out for themselves – it must be pointed out

Put it over effectively

Your careful preparations will do much to ensure that your training sessions are a success. However, at least as much will depend on *you* and how you go about the job. The foundation for a rewarding training session is your own self-preparation. This should include these actions a day or two before D-Day:

■ Ensure that your own notes are complete and in the right

order
- Check that handouts are all present and correct, that each is compatible with the other and that you know at which point in the session you will use them
- Go through your notes and rehearse what you are going to say – ideally you will be able to speak fluently and with confidence with only an occasional glance at your notes
- Look over any sample documents or other visual aids to ensure that you are fully familiar with them and will not be caught wondering what something means or is used for

Attention to this kind of detail is vital. You may have extensive knowledge of your subject but any small foul-up during the training can sap your confidence and even make you look silly.

Training other people can be a thoroughly rewarding and enjoyable experience – if you take a lot of trouble to get the nuts and bolts right.

Your method and style

Your method of putting it over should take account of obstacles to learning which will stand in the way of the trainees. These obstacles will include:

- Boredom
- Fatigue
- Fear
- Distraction
- Sense of irrelevance
- Too highbrow
- Too lowbrow
- Too fast – or too slow

Some of these obstacles will be broken down by your preparation but your delivery must not be such that it builds them up again. These are some fundamental ways and means to make your training sessions easy to assimilate:

Start gently with some relatively 'neutral' remarks

A few minutes can be spent on the general administration (tea breaks and the like) and a general reminder of the purpose of the training. This will help to settle both you and the trainees down.

The way in which the session is to be conducted can also be explained. For example: that you will be showing a film, that handouts will be provided, that you expect the trainees to participate and so on.

Keep it lively

A dreary monotonous speaker can bore his audience to death and make it hard work to listen to him.

Remember:

- Be enthusiastic – if you indicate that you find the whole thing a bit of a bind or an irritating interruption to your normal work you cannot blame the trainees for taking a similar attitude
- Put some humour in it – while business should be taken seriously there is no reason for it to be taken solemnly. A few light-hearted remarks can reduce tension and will help to make things palatable

  You may make a mistake. If so, this is a golden opportunity to make a joke *against yourself*. Having a dig at yourself will help to remove any barriers between you and the trainees and will keep them listening
- Get the trainees talking. Ask for their opinions and encourage them to discuss the subject you are covering. Participation helps to reduce both boredom and fatigue

Don't go on too long without a break
Your trainees will have physical needs for a break including hunger, thirst and the need to use a lavatory. Give regular opportunities to meet these needs – no one can concentrate with the distraction of a full bladder.

Fatigue will also take its toll – especially if you are doing a lot of talking. Ways to keep fatigue down include:

■ Giving the trainees a mini-exercise or allowing them to practise what you have taught
■ A demonstration, a film or any other visual means of communication. In addition to easing fatigue, a visual method makes learning more effective. We remember what we have seen better than things we have heard
■ A visit to something away from the training area. Even a few minutes looking at the warehouse loading bay or the company computer room will be a great help. The physical exercise (however little) and the change of scenery relieves mental fatigue

Remember, no session should go on for more than about 40 minutes without a break. Stick to your starting and finishing times.

Be patient, understanding and friendly
A friendly relationship with your trainees will help them to learn. Fear of you – or of failure – adds stress and positively discourages learning.

The trainer must be encouraging and supportive, never lose his temper and never issue threats.

Sarcasm and humiliating comments have no place in the professional trainer's repertoire. Remember how you have felt if you have ever been at the receiving end of snide remarks – especially if you have done your best.

Be prepared to:

■ Go over the work again willingly if needed. The chances are that if the trainees are having difficulty it means that your teaching has been poor!

■ Slow down or otherwise adjust your programme to suit the trainees' needs

■ Ask the trainees what is bothering them and act accordingly

■ Take the blame if there are difficulties: 'Sorry, I did not do a very good job of explaining that point' is a statement which will take the stress off the trainees, encourage them and gain you the respect you need. It is also likely to be true that you did not do a very good job. Even if you did, be big enough to take the blame

Work at the trainees' level
It is easy to overestimate the level of understanding of your group. Subjects that appear easy to the trainer often do so because of long experience with them. The trainee may, as a result of little or no experience, have great difficulty in understanding the subject.

As soon as a trainee fails to grasp something you have lost him. Once lost the trainee is likely to switch off and get deeper and deeper into difficulty.

Such problems can be avoided by:

■ Going fairly slowly. Never rush things – too fast a delivery inhibits learning

■ Ask questions to check understanding as you go along. Make sure that a subject is understood before going on to the next

■ Explain all technical terms and jargon. Translate initials such as E O Q (Economic Order Quality) and D C F (Discounted Cash Flow)

A cardinal rule is *never* to use the training session as a means to demonstrate your own knowledge. One company trainer wasted many hours of valuable time and demoralized his trainees by showing off. The purpose of the training was to explain and clarify some basic legal principles to trainees with no legal training. The trainer, a lawyer, went on an ego trip with complicated scenarios and terminology which the trainees did not understand. The trainer enjoyed the sessions; the trainees did not and they learned very little.

It is of course possible to underestimate the trainees' knowledge and bore them with information they already have. The author experienced this problem when improperly briefed about the knowledge level of a group. The ideas and material used were already familiar to most of the trainees and a morning was wasted before this was discovered. The trainees felt insulted and the author embarrassed! This problem can be avoided by carefully checking the trainees' level *before* preparing the material.

Re-cap and allow practice
The old adage 'Tell them what you are going to say, say it and then tell them what you have said' holds good in training. At the end of each topic summarize the key points. Then, if it is appropriate, get the trainees to practise what has been taught. Both the summary and the practice will help to reinforce the learning.

Make it realistic
Exercises should be as close to real life as possible – ideally they will be taken *from* real life. Likewise any examples that you use should be real ones although sometimes a contrived example is unavoidable.

Keeping the work close to reality will underline the relevance of the training to the company and the trainees.

Stimulate curiosity
Curiosity is a powerful factor in gaining the attention of a

trainee. At the beginning of a lecture – or even an after-dinner speech – the listener will normally be paying close attention to the speaker. This is due to a sense of curiosity – 'What is this fellow going to say?', 'Are we to hear something exciting?', 'What kind of person is this?' – and the like.

Once the curiosity is satisfied attention drifts away unless some other stimulating factor such as an exercise or a demonstration is introduced. Alternatively the trainer can seek ways to re-introduce the curiosity factor from time to time as he goes along. Ways to do this include:

- Covering up something to come. Suppose that the trainer is dealing with a series of points or topics. Instead of writing up an appropriate series of headings on a flip chart, or showing them on a slide, he can cover up all but the ones he has dealt with or is dealing with. Strips of paper stuck onto a flip chart, covering the headings, will indicate to the trainees that more is to come. There will be curiosity as to what it is. The strips can be removed one by one as the teaching proceeds with a stimulus to attention each time.

  This technique also has the advantage of concentrating the trainees' minds on the subject being dealt with. If all the headings are visible from the start, at least some of the trainees will be pondering the ones not being talked about.
- Having a model, a piece of equipment or some other object to be used later, placed in front of the trainees but covered with a cloth. The effect is similar to that of the strips covering headings on a flip chart – the trainees will be curious about what is to come. Some trainers prefer to have the object uncovered but to say nothing about it until they are ready to use it. If then a trainee says 'What is that?' or 'What is that thing for?' the trainer can reply, mysteriously, 'You will see'.
- Bringing in another speaker to deal with part of the subject. This could be someone from outside the company or some

other person the trainees do not know. The change of speaker will revive the curiosity present at the start of the session with the 'What is he going to say?' effect.

Be careful with handouts

There is a danger that if notes or other handouts are distributed at the beginning of a session the trainees will spend their time reading them and not listening to you. For this reason it is often better to give them out at the end of the session. There are however times when it is helpful to give the trainees a handout during the course of the talk.

A diagram, a photograph or some other illustration of what you are talking about can be used to clarify what you are putting over – indeed it is sometimes close to impossible to describe something accurately and effectively without such a visual aid to help the trainees. A short list of points to be made is something else which can sometimes be usefully handed out. You can then take the class through the points one by one. The list will aid the memory of the trainees and help to focus their minds on the points you are making – providing there are not so many that you lose their attention while they are looking down the page. Four or five points are enough – so that they can be taken in at a glance.

Watch out for the awkward squad

It is not unknown to have a disruptive character in your group. The argumentative character, the guy who wants to show off and the comedian are all familiar to trainers. The golden rule in dealing with these people is 'Do not get into a conflict with them'. The difficult personality likes nothing better than to take over the session by provoking the trainer into an argument or making him lose his temper. The result can be catastrophic and exhausting for the trainer. A good technique is to let the group deal with the trouble-maker.

One experienced trainer recognized, early on in a session,

that one of the trainees was likely to be a problem. The trainee made one or two politically motivated comments and the trainer guessed, correctly, that the comments were feelers to see how the trainer would react. He expected a more forceful and militant comment to be made later and sure enough it was.

Instead of risking a confrontation with the trainee the trainer merely turned to the group and said 'You have heard Charlie's remark, what do *you* think?'

The group demolished Charlie's remark in double quick time.

The fact is that the vast majority of trainees *want* to learn (especially if the 'reason why' has been properly explained) and do not want some smart Alec to ruin the session. They also become bored with smart Alecs and, after a time, are only too pleased to put them down.

Another approach is to take the problem trainee to one side during a break and have a word with him. This should be done privately and the rest of the trainees should not be aware of it. You can then state quite firmly that you will not accept his disruptive behaviour and, if it continues, you will ask him to leave. It must be made very clear that you are in charge and intend to stay that way. Whatever the case don't beg or try to appeal to the trouble-maker's better nature. Any approach along such lines may well encourage him in his disruption.

This firm line should be taken even when the trainee is senior to you in the company hierarchy. This takes courage but the alternative could be a disastrous training session which will do no good to your long-term reputation.

Practise, practise, practise

Awareness of the factors described combined with careful preparation can make you into a workmanlike trainer. Real skill, as with other types of work, comes with practice. If your first attempt is a bit shaky don't give up – your next effort will be better. Get all the practice you can, however brief or insignificant each session may be – it all counts.

Follow up – get reactions

In addition to any long-term follow-up to your training it can be valuable to obtain the views of the trainees promptly after the course is completed or, if they are widely spaced, after each session.

This can be done by brief interviews but a more effective method is to use a post-course assessment form. A copy of the form is handed to each trainee at the end of the training with the instruction to complete and return it within 24 hours. The objective is to obtain their reaction while everything is fresh in their minds. The results can be valuable in assessing your performance and the methods you used. N.B. some trainees will be reluctant to make adverse remarks about a trainer – especially if he is the boss. For this reason you may prefer to let the trainees complete their forms anonymously.

The form must be designed to suit your particular situation but something like this is suggested:

POST COURSE ASSESSMENT FORM		
COURSE:	TRAINER:	DATE OF COURSE:
How much did you think you needed this course before you attended it? ☐ HIGH ☐ MEDIUM ☐ LOW		
How much do you think you needed it having attended it? ☐ HIGH ☐ MEDIUM ☐ LOW		
How do you rate the following? (please rate on a scale of 1 = poor to 10 = excellent) EXPLANATORY COMMENTS THE PRESENTER ☐ THE HANDOUTS ☐		

VISUAL AIDS ☐
PRACTICAL WORK ☐
LOCATION ☐
TIME ALLOWED ☐
FILMS/VIDEOS ☐
OTHER (Please state) ☐

What would you suggest as an improvement to the course?

Who else should attend this course and why?

The answers to the questions on the form should be carefully studied. The first question will give you some idea of the attitudes of the trainees before the training. If, for instance, a number of them feel that they had a 'low' need for training it may indicate that either your pre-course communication was poor or that there is a general lack of motivation and some complacency – or a combination of these.

If the answers to the second question reveal that the trainees believe, post-course, that their need was 'high' then you will know that you are hitting a worthwhile target.

The scores for such aspects as the handouts, visual aids etc., will indicate where you need to do some homework and any suggestions received should be carefully considered.

A CHECKLIST FOR WOULD-BE TRAINERS

1. Have you clearly defined the objective of the training?
2. Have the trainees been selected on the basis of genuine need for the training?
3. Have the trainees been fully briefed and do they know the objective? Do they see how the training will benefit them in future?
4. Is all the preparation done?:

- Place
- Handouts
- Visual Aids
- Your notes
- Equipment
- Exercises
- Demonstrations

5. Are you fully prepared yourself – fully familiar with the subject and ready to put it over confidently, fluently and in a readily assimilable way?

The various forms of training open to you

By no means every training session involves a classroom, a lecturer and a class. A number of other methods can be used with advantages attached to each.

On-job-training

This method has two distinct advantages – it overcomes the time problem ('I have no time to teach my staff') and it can be effectively used when there are too few trainees to make up a group.

A further advantage can be gained from the fact that if cleverly organized OJT can result in productive work from the trainee at an early stage.

What is OJT?

There is a lot of misunderstanding as to what OJT really is. The most common mistake is to assume it is a kind of 'learn as you go along' technique requiring little or no planning, structure or follow-up. Someone told to watch what Fred does or join in and pick it up is not being given OJT. Such methods are time consuming, almost always ineffective and sometimes downright damaging. The chances are that watching what Fred does will result in learning all the mistakes that Fred makes and perpetuating them.

Real OJT can be best explained by describing how it works.

The starting point for OJT is the setting up of an objective as explained earlier. The need for a clear objective is no less important with OJT than with any other form of training.

In addition, the other basic requirements must be met such as explanation to the trainee as to what it is all about. Having prepared the ground, the following steps can be taken:

(1) The subject to be taught is carefully defined. This could be say, processing an order from a customer.

(2) The subject to be taught is now broken down into segments. Processing an order might involve the following segments:

■ Checking for credit clearance
■ Confirming product descriptions and codes
■ Completion of internal forms for despatch and accounts departments
■ Recording the order on a customer record

(3) The time required to teach each segment is now estimated and a training timetable drawn up which allows for the teaching of each segment and a suitable amount of practising time.

The programme might look something like this:

ON-JOB TRAINING PROGRAMME		
Subject: Sales Order Entry	Trainee: F. Smith	Trainer: B. Jones
Date	Subject	Time
1st June	Credit clearance	30 mins.
2nd June	Supervised practice	
3rd June	Product descriptions and codes	20 mins.
4th June	Supervised practice	
5th June	Internal forms	25 mins.
8th June	Re-cap and progress check	25 mins.
9th June	Supervised practice	
10th June	Customer record entries	15 mins.
11th June	Supervised practice	
12th June	Final re-cap and progress check	30 mins.

Such a programme demands only brief periods of the trainer's time yet, at the end of two weeks, the whole job has been taught.

The supervised practice achieves two important goals:

■ The trainee's learning is reinforced
■ The trainee is actually producing something

The result of only a brief training session is a contribution to the work of the department which, apart from its profit value to the company, will be encouraging to the trainee. As the programme goes on the trainee will be adding more skills to his repertoire and increasing his contribution.

Taking the work in small, digestible bits is easier for both trainee and trainer as there is less to be learned and taught at a time than if the whole job was tackled in one lengthy session.

The programme must however be adhered to in a disciplined way. The trainer must set aside the time required for the sessions – and stick to them. The best way is to start each session at the same time each day (say 9.00 a.m.) so that they become routine. Any session skipped or postponed will wreck the whole thing and demoralize the trainee. For this reason it may be helpful to have a reserve trainer for *genuine* emergencies such as the appointed trainer going sick. However, reserve trainers should never be used because it is 'convenient' – consistency in the style and content of the training is important and should be maintained.

Don't forget the follow-up
OJT, like any other form of training, must be followed up. However good the planning and preparation may be, however conscientious the trainer and trainee, things can go wrong. Checks must be made to see that:

- The timetable has been adhered to
- The trainee has not become stuck due to an over-ambitious programme or for other reasons
- Trainer and trainee have confidence in each other and have not fallen out

It is also possible that as the training has gone along some new factor has come to light which means that a change of programme timing or content is desirable. If this is so don't hesitate to discuss the programme with the trainee and make appropriate changes. Training plans should never be carved on granite tablets.

Exposure training

It is not uncommon to find situations where a promising employee is earmarked for higher things – and sent on a round-trip of the company departments. It is also a common feature of these 'spend a bit of time in each department' plans that little that is useful results.

Such failures are avoidable if a few simple precautions are taken.

The first requirement is to recognize that training by exposure to a variety of situations and problems also needs to be planned – in detail and with set objectives.

The following requirements must be met:

- The overall purpose of the exercise must be clear and expressed, in writing, in terms of an objective against which progress can be measured. Something like this is required: 'Smith is to be prepared to take over the Timbuktu office on 1 March 1992. By 1 January 1992 Smith must be able to:
  (1) carry out all office procedures
  (2) instruct and supervise local staff in carrying out local procedures
  (3) negotiate with local customs officers and deal with export/import documentation
  (4) be fully familiar with stock-holding and warehousing activities including space allocation and economic order calculations – and so on.
- The overall requirement must be broken down into specific training to be received in appropriate departments.

  For example, the office procedures which Smith has to learn must be precisely identified e.g.
  (1) Invoice and credit note preparation
  (2) Control of debtors
  (3) Banking procedures
  (4) Preparation and transmission of sales reports
  (5) Stock valuation

  This detailed breakdown will act as a checklist against which learning can be compared. The trainee will actually practise the skills and, by working in the department concerned, be *exposed* to the general background and environment. Thus he will be faced with situations involving, say, disgruntled customers, computer breakdowns and other 'environmental problems'. When he works in the warehouse to learn space allocation and the like he will be exposed to problems of lack of forklift trucks, errors in positioning of stock, unexplained return of some goods and all the other background matters which are 'non-standard', difficult to forecast yet require managing

■ To help ensure that the training is effective separate objectives will be required for the work to be done in *each* department. These objectives will list all the specific tasks to be learned and may, in addition, have a catch-all clause for the unusual e.g. 'and will be involved in the solving of emergency or unexpected problems and be made aware of any non-routine situations which may arise'.

■ A detailed programme must be drawn up to include all the work to be learned, showing who is responsible for teaching each subject and by when.

This provision will make it possible to monitor progress. In addition the programme, which *must* be constructed with the aid of those who will do the training, will act as a check that nothing essential has been left out.

Important also is provision in each departmental programme for regular 'chat sessions'. In one real-life case these sessions, between the trainee and the head of the department, took place every Friday afternoon – without fail. The sessions included:

- a review of the work done during the week with additional explanation where required
- questions and answers
- explanations of general background, history, legal aspects, potential future developments, etc

The chat sessions allow flesh to be put on the bones of the routines and to put them in the context of the departmental or company operation as a whole.

Similarly, much can be gained by involving the trainee in meetings either in or out of the department. Valuable

exposure can be gained by:
- accompanying a sales manager during a visit to a customer
- attending a meeting with the company bankers
- involvement in sales and production liaison meetings
- observing at a board meeting

These and other situations can bring out aspects of the job which are difficult to specify in advance but are nevertheless very real.

Some positive don'ts

1. Don't fail to *plan* the exposure programme.

2. Don't fail to communicate the plan to all concerned with the 'reasons why'.

3. Don't assume that departmental managers will automatically welcome the trainee and do a good job of teaching him. This must be assured by the plan, monitoring it and involving the departments in the planning and the monitoring.

4. Don't assume that just sitting in the department concerned for a few days will do the trick – it will not.

5. Don't leave it all to the trainee. One unfortunate trainee arrived at a factory in Wales on the first port of call of his exposure programme to be faced with an obviously uninterested and slightly hostile manager.

'What do you want to know?' asked the manager.

The trainee, unable to answer the question with any precision (*because* he was a trainee) was then told: 'If you can't tell me what you want to know there is not much I can do about it'.

The trainee was then left to his own devices, drifting around the department until he went back to his boss to explain the problem. The whole process then had to start again.

6. Don't allow the old sweats to use the 'I've been in this job for twenty years' ploy.

Some people believe, quite seriously, that it takes a lifetime to learn their jobs. This is almost always nonsense and a whopping case of self-delusion with a modicum of ego boosting built in. Yes, it can be depressing to admit that a bright trainee can pick up the guts of a job in a few weeks or months but it frequently happens to be true.

Each job has a learning curve which is normally shaped like this:

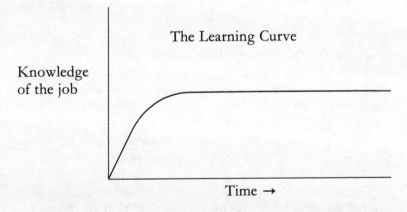

The Learning Curve

Knowledge of the job

Time →

Most of the knowledge required is taken on board at a rapid pace during the early stages. The learning process then slows down and, although we never stop learning, the later years involve relatively little in the way of new information.

However, the later years are ones in which an almost instinctive skill is acquired as a result of much practice and it is this which the old sweats can confuse with knowledge.

This confusion must not be a barrier to exposure learning since it is not true for someone to say: 'You can't learn this job in a few months – it has taken me twenty years to get where I am.'

The second part of this statement may be true but that does not make the first part true as well.

When should exposure training be used?

In addition to preparation for a new task such as taking over the Timbuktu office exposure training can be useful in other cases:

Fast track people

The growth of a company from say 50 employees to 100 or 150 often requires the introduction of a different kind of employee into the business.

A company which could manage its affairs quite comfortably with the old, possibly ageing, team may now require some specialist skills. The new type of employee might be one or more of:

- A qualified accountant to add more sophisticated know-how and procedures to what has hitherto been a bookkeeping department.

  Tax, investment and budgeting questions may now be arising on a regular basis and rather than referring such matters to an outside firm of accountants it may be more sensible to place the necessary skills in-house
- A specialist engineer to sharpen up quality control, improve productivity or inject some new know-how into research and development
- A professional marketing man with experience of particular markets which the company wishes to penetrate

The value to the company of all such people is rarely fully achieved until they have a good all round knowledge of what goes on in the business – and its culture. They will need to know who *really* calls the shots, the hallowed traditions, the sacred cows ('the MD will not countenance the use of plastic in any of the company products') and all the other environmental influences.

The company paperwork, production lead times, financial policy and restraints are also the sort of knowledge which a specialist newcomer will need to acquire. A specially tailored exposure training plan can provide the knowledge quickly.

Project team members

If the company is intending to expand by acquisition, diversify, or start up a subsidiary, such developments are often best handled by a project team.

While a well balanced team will include all the necessary specialists, the more the team members understand about each others' jobs and the overall operation the better the result is likely to be.

Exposure training, again tailored to the individual, can provide the necessary breadth of knowledge and understanding required.

Future directors

Mention has already been made of the need for training prior to taking a seat in the boardroom. Directors must stop concentrating on their past areas of interest and expertise and take an overview of the business as a whole, and they will need to be equipped to do so. Some time spent in each department looking at what goes on and learning what the problems are can be a valuable asset when deliberating company strategy.

WARNING: The fact that someone is to become a director does not mean that his status makes study of the detail unnecessary. Be careful to avoid the trap of sending potential directors on a round of lunches and cosy chats with other senior people. This is likely to be a waste of time and will result in little knowledge of any real value being gained. Make it a 'hands-on' exercise as it should be for everyone else.

A variation on exposure training

A longer-term exposure training plan can be organized on the basis of job rotation.

This can involve several people or just one. The idea is to give the people concerned a spell *fully acting* in a particular role for say, six months and then moving them on to another area.

In one real-life case a person destined to take over a small subsidiary company followed the following programme:

- Assistant distribution manager – 6 months
- Assistant General Manager – 3 months
- Assistant Company Secretary – 3 months

These roles exposed the trainee to aspects of the business of which he had limited knowledge and gave him some hands-on experience – problems and all.

Discovery training

A little-known technique, discovery training has great value in certain situations. There are occasions when something has to be done which has never been done before and for which there are few guidelines. Such cases occur from time to time in the clothing industry.

A company may have been making garments for many years when along comes a customer who wants something quite different from the garments made in the past. How to cut the material (economically as well as efficiently), how to assemble the pieces, how to use the sewing-machines, add the trimmings and so on needs to be worked out.

This sorting out job could be attempted by managers who, having worked out what they think is the best way, must train the cutters, machinists and finishers.

The chances are that there will be an element of the blind

leading the blind with a number of false starts and returns to the drawing board.

The alternative is discovery learning. In the case of garment-making one sample of the required garment will be handmade and given to a small team of machinists, cutters or whatever. They will be provided with the raw materials and asked to work out how best to do the job of getting from raw material to finished article.

This method – leaving the employees to 'discover' the best way to tackle a job – can cause some of the more traditional and conservative managers to throw up their hands in horror. However, fears that management is abdicating its authority and responsibility and that industrial anarchy (at least) is just around the corner are misplaced. Discovery training has many advantages.

The advantages of discovery training

(1) The employees will look for the easiest way to do the job. This will often be the least costly in labour time.

(2) The employees will be committed to *their* method and are unlikely to vary it once they have worked it out.

(3) The employees will be proud of their achievement and will be motivated. They will want to make it a success if *they* have thought of it.

(4) The practical skills of the employees will be utilized in the discovery process i.e. any work method decided upon will be a practicable proposition – not always the case when someone else specifies how to do the job.

(5) There will be no griping about 'this daft idea that "they" have imposed on us'.

Management's role should be to:

- Set standards of quality and quantity
- Monitor what is going on but to avoid interfering
- Encourage but not criticize
- Give praise where it is due

Kits to help you

Do-it-yourself training can be greatly assisted by the use of a variety of kits available from various sources. These are primarily 'self-teach' systems involving the use of videos, computer disks, audiotapes and work books.

They are useful when a series of people require training, one at a time, over a long period and there is never an opportunity to put them together in a training group.

Most kits are designed to be used with a 'mentor' who will guide and assist the trainee and monitor progress. Some are 'interactive' in that the trainee will be tested by the system as he goes along and his responses will be evaluated. The system may then repeat work done which the trainee has not fully understood or take him along a different path until he is ready to move on to a new stage.

Some trainees respond particularly well to this form of training – often because the trainee controls the speed himself and any mistakes he makes are not visible to other people.

More details of self-teach kits are provided in Appendix II.

D.I.Y. training – with outside trainers

Obtaining an outsider to do your training may seem to be a contradiction of the do-it-yourself principle. It is however a hybrid approach which still leaves the whole thing under your control and can meet a number of specific needs.

Bringing in an outside trainer can be particularly helpful when:

■ The skills required do not exist in-house but you do not wish to send trainees on external courses – or suitable courses cannot be found
■ The situation is urgent and you have no time to train the trainers or design the training
■ It is believed that an outsider will have more impact on the trainees than familiar faces within the company
■ Your own situation and needs are such that you require a tailor-made course for your people which includes particular know-how which a particular outsider can provide

There are a number of companies and individuals who will provide you with training on your premises to your specification.

What a good outside trainer will do

In addition to running effectively the training sessions that you require a truly professional trainer will carry out the following preliminary work:

■ Review with you the objectives that you have in mind and the type of training you feel necessary.
     The trainer, based on his experience, may propose alternatives or amendments to your ideas. This can be especially valuable if your own training experience is limited
■ Obtain a brief from you – if necessary the brief can be drafted jointly – to ensure that there is no doubt as to what is to be taught to whom and when
■ Interview a representative sample of the trainees to ascertain their attitudes and existing level of knowledge
■ Acquire a basic knowledge of your company (size, products, markets), the environment in which it operates and

how the proposed training fits into your plans for the future

Equipped with this knowledge the trainer will design a package of training to suit your needs. He should then produce for you a programme of sessions for your approval and possibly some sample handouts or other material so that you can check the level and quality of the work.

A professional trainer can also assist you with the selection of outside venues (if required) and with follow-up work.

Please don't ask him to write confidential reports on your trainees. Somehow or other the trainees will get to know of it and there will be a resulting barrier between trainer and trainees. The trainer will be working to develop a rapport between himself and the people he is teaching. In particular he will be establishing a state of trust so that trainees will not be afraid to reveal their difficulties to him. This will not happen if the threat of a confidential report is lurking about, and the training will not take place in a relaxed atmosphere.

You can, of course, ask the trainer to recommend any further training that he thinks will be of benefit to a trainee and/or provide comments on the strengths of individuals which might be put to better use in the future. This constructive analysis can be conducted in face-to-face discussions with managers – a process which is almost always more helpful and meaningful than a few words in a confidential report.

Choosing your outside trainer

Merely because a trainer is employed by a large and illustrious firm of consultants does not necessarily mean that he is right for you or your trainees.

The person you need will have the following attributes:

- A successful teaching style
- A sound knowledge of the subject

- A 'working' knowledge of your industry sufficient for him to be able to put the training into the context of the trainees' jobs.
- A *detailed* knowledge of your industry is not likely to be necessary – sales technique, for example, does not vary greatly between industries – providing the trainer is aware of your type of market and the segment that you deal in.

  Leadership skills, communication techniques and computer skills are also little affected by the type of industry. However, a good trainer will check the environment and pick up any genuine differences that he must allow for
- A personality and general appearance which appeals to you and is likely to appeal to the trainees. This is a matter for your judgement

How to confirm that the trainer is right for you is not always easy but the following steps can be taken:

- Ask for and take up references with former clients
- Ask for evidence of the trainer's knowledge and experience. He should be able to provide it

If in any doubt, a limited training job can be arranged and the results checked. If you are satisfied with this trial the trainer can be given further work.

SUMMARY OF KEY POINTS

1. There are positive advantages in do-it-yourself training but you must, first, train your trainers.

2. Successful D.I.Y. training depends upon:
- Careful planning and preparation (e.g. defining the objectives of the training).
- Choosing the right techniques (e.g. visual aids)
- Getting the detail right
- Using a teaching style which encourages learning

3. Training sessions should be formally followed up to ensure that you are getting value for money.

4. In addition to classroom training the following methods are available:
- On-job training
- Exposure training (and job rotation)
- Discovery training

5. There are a number of D.I.Y. training kits which can help you.

6. An outside trainer can be helpful on the inside.

CHAPTER SIX

Using External Training Services

THERE IS A massive choice of external training facilities available to you. They range from the excellent to the dreadful. There is, within the range, almost certain to be something appropriate to your needs and much that is not.

One of the biggest problems for companies wishing to use external training courses is finding high quality and appropriate offerings from the mass that is available. Fortunately there are ways and means to reduce the chance of wasting time and money.

Why, though, should you consider external training at all?

The potential benefits of external training courses

Assuming that the right course has been chosen the benefits will include the following – in addition to the fact that the trainee should learn what you want him to learn:

■ *Exposure to people from other companies.* The ideas and experience of people working in other companies (possibly other industries) can be very valuable. The trainee will probably discover that other companies than his own have similar problems and that there are ways and means to deal with them. He will also very probably be stimulated by discussion with people from other environments and *made to think.* He is not likely to achieve the same stimulation from colleagues in his own company with whom he will be familiar, who have opinions which he has heard over and over again and who are influenced by the same company culture and background as himself.

■ *Awareness of techniques and approaches to problems used by other industries which, with appropriate adjustment, can be applied in his own company.* An example was the manager in a firm of insurance brokers who attended a one week course on basic management skills. His first reaction was that the course was a waste of time because the material and examples used were largely taken from manufacturing industries.

However, after a time he realized that production scheduling, job costing and similar techniques could be applied in a broker's office as well as in, say, an engineering company. He introduced such techniques into his own work with marked success – in particular speeding up the flow and improving the control of paperwork.

It is noteworthy that in this case a common barrier was broken down by an external course. This is the barrier which people create for themselves and express in the time-honoured statement 'We are different'.

A good trainer will help the delegates on his course to gain maximum benefit by encouraging discussion and cross-fertilization of ideas. He will also, if teaching management techniques, explain how they can be used in a variety of ways in a variety of businesses.

The disadvantages of external training

If you have chosen the right course the main disadvantage, compared with doing it yourself, is cost.

However, when comparing costs the time of your own internal trainer should be taken into account. This often narrows the gap considerably.

There is also the disadvantage that the course may not take account of any cultural or other peculiarities of your company.

Cultural factors can be crucial in determining the usefulness of external training. A major British company arranged for a series of managers to attend courses on leadership and man-management. The result was a conflict between the 'liberal' ideas taught on the course and the highly autocratic and centralized style of management which dominated its own culture. Trainees were returning from the course convinced of the advantages of delegation (for example) and placing decision-making powers at lower levels in the hierarchy. They were also attracted by ideas favouring the encouragement of lower-level participation and entrepreneurial thinking. Such notions were so far removed from the long-held idea at the top of the company that employees needed to be controlled and driven that confusion was just about the only result of the training. Of course, if the top brass had taken the course first the result might have been very different!

Why should you opt for external training?

The most obvious reason for deciding on external training is that you are unable to do it yourself. However, there are other situations which might influence your decision:

- *When the external course is used to form part of an exposure learning programme.* In this case the trainee is being deliberately placed in a wholly different environment and exposed to new thinking
- *When 'new blood' is required.* You could be stuck in a rut and some entrepreneurial thinking is needed. Trainees will often come back from a course bubbling with ideas. The ideas are not necessarily earth-shattering, they could be quite mundane, but they are not so likely to come to the surface in the familiar (and perhaps pressured) situation in the company. A good external course can make people think.
- *When new attitudes are needed.* The attitudes of people – to their company, colleagues and work – can be markedly improved by the effects of an external course. One case involved an

administrator who was well known for being bloody-minded and difficult to get on with.

On the pretext that he was required to vet a course for his company he was sent away to learn negotiation skills.

He came back much changed and was later heard to remark that he was surprised how much the atmosphere in the company had changed. 'Everyone', he said 'has become more reasonable'!

So there are distinct benefits to be gained – providing you can pick the right course for you and your trainees.

What then do you have to choose from?

The courses available to you

Possibly the most frequently available are the one or two-day courses – often described as seminars. Such seminars are offered by a multitude of organizations including well known and well-established ones such as the Industrial Society. There are also less prominent organizations who may well offer equally high-quality courses – particularly if they specialize in one particular topic. However there is some poor material on the market to be avoided.

The one and two-day courses cover subjects such as:

- Employment law
- Sales technique
- Telephone skills
- Secretarial skills
- Presentation technique
- Time management
- Delegation
- Safety at work

Longer courses – one to three weeks – are available at business schools such as Cranfield School of Management (Bedfordshire) and the polytechnics. The longer courses cover such topics as:

- Marketing strategy
- Management and Leadership skills
- Corporate Planning
- Organization and Methods techniques
- Accounting for non-accountants

Distance Learning

A variation on the theme of external courses are 'distance learning' courses available from the Open University and other seats of learning. Keele University, for example, offers a ten-month course on Information Technology. The student works at home using electronic communication with the university – which issues a certificate on satisfactory completion of the course. 'Distance learning' is the modern equivalent of the old correspondence course.

How to go about finding the right courses

A good starting point is to make contact with a *reputable* body providing courses or which may give you sound advice. The following are reliable sources of advice, training or both:

- The Industrial Society (Peter Runge House, 3, Carlton House Terrace, London SW1Y 5DG, Tel. 071–839 4300)
- The British Institute of Management (Management House, Cottingham Rd., Corby, Northants. Tel. Corby 204222)
- The business schools
- Local Productivity Associations – such as the Bucks and East Berks Productivity Association Limited (4A, Albert

St., Windsor, Berks. SL4 5BV, Tel: 0753 831031)
- Your local polytechnic
- The Institute of Personnel Management (IPM House, Camp Rd., Wimbledon SW19 4UX)
- The Chartered Institute of Arbitrators (75, Cannon St., London EC4N 5BH Tel: 071–236 8761)
- The Institute of Chartered Accountants (Moorgate Place, London EC2P 2BJ Tel: 071–628 7060)
- The Institute of Freight Forwarders (8 Paradise Rd., Richmond Surrey TW9 13A Tel: 081–948 3141)
- Department of Trade and Industry – regional offices
- Local Development agencies
- Local Chambers of Commerce
- The Chartered Institute of Marketing (Moor Hall, Cookham, Maidenhead, Berks SL6 9QH, Tel: 0628 524922)

Having obtained details of courses provided or recommended by organizations such as those listed – not forgetting your own trade or professional association if not included in the list – the next step is to study the course *content* carefully. The *title* of the course may not tell you very much and may in fact be misleading.

What do the course titles mean?

Some course titles, particularly those chosen by certain commercial organizations, are nothing more than the training equivalent of the misleading picture on the cover of a book. These titles are traps for the unwary. However even some wholly respectable titles may be confusing to you if you are not familiar with the jargon. The following are in current use:

- *Action Centred Leadership*. This training, offered by the Industrial Society, deals with the need for managers to concentrate on the three areas of 'The Task' to be accomplished, 'The Team' being managed and 'The Individual' employee. How to achieve this balance and how success depends on it is the subject of the course

■ *Inter-personal skills*. These courses vary in content but are perhaps best described as 'how to be diplomatic and get on with people'.

They may suit negotiators and sales people as well as managers at all levels whose success depends on cooperation and constructive personal relationships with others. These courses would be valuable to politicians such as those representing the EEC countries!

■ *Corporate Planning*. How to look ahead, make forecasts of market trends and the like and prepare a plan of action for your company. A number of statistical and other techniques may be included. A useful result of corporate planning training is the awareness of how important it is to plan ahead – and how dangerous it can be to work on a day-to-day or week-to-week basis

■ *Human Resource Strategies*. These courses vary in emphasis but normally deal with training and development planning for your people, motivation, manpower planning, salary schemes and almost anything else that can affect your people and their contribution to the company

■ *Operations Research*. Sometimes termed Operational Research, this topic covers mathematical techniques for solving problems. Applications of O.R. include calculation of machine capacity required to meet a varying workload (economically), sales forecasting, optimum use of vehicles or other equipment and the 'mix' of products to achieve maximum profits. Some mathematical skill is needed to cope with the subject

■ *Creativity*. The word creativity is likely to appear amongst others in the title of the course e.g.

'Creativity for first-line managers'
'Unlocking your creative abilities'
'Creativity – the key to profit'

'How to be creative'

Normally these courses teach a variety of techniques for coming up with new ideas. Brain-storming is one such technique. They have value for people regularly faced with difficult decisions or intractable problems in addition to those responsible for future entrepreneurial action

- *Employee Counselling.* This activity is not the same as appraisal interviewing since it deals with specific employee problems such as alcoholism, drug-taking, debts and the like. There are courses available on how to approach and advise employees with such problems, with the aim of helping them and keeping them as valuable employees

- *Total Quality Management.* A popular expression, T.Q.M. is familiar to old hands in management training as 'team-work'.

  Now presented as a philosophy, T.Q.M. asks its fans to adopt attitudes such as finishing the job before going home, supporting colleagues in difficulties, picking up work which someone else has overlooked and so on.

- *Financial Appreciation.* Sometimes this subject is more clearly described as 'Financial skills for non-financial managers' or similar.

  Contents may include:
  - how to read a balance sheet
  - budgeting
  - cash flow forecasting
  - break-even calculation
  - investment (e.g. ways to calculate return on investment)
  - raising capital

  A good course covering these subjects can greatly enhance the potential of future directors who have no day-to-day involvement in finance (e.g. sales and personnel managers) and most senior people working in a non-financial area

- *Information Technology (I.T.).* Essentially this is 'how to use computers effectively in your business'.

No-one seems to know how I.T. (as it is popularly known) gained its title. However, it reflects the realization that the role of computers in business is to provide fast and accurate information rather than carry out complex calculations. Data such as stock levels and values, work in progress, cash flow forecasts and sales volumes are the valuable results of a computer system. I.T. courses, which vary enormously in content, deal with ways and means to use your computer to produce the information you want effectively to control your business.

An example is the growing use of computers in point-of-sale applications. The till at the retail shop check-out is linked to a central computer. Every purchase is 'captured' at the point-of-sale and the computer records the cash received and re-calculates the stock levels. This enables management to monitor revenue and volume of sales and to re-order at the right time to replenish stocks

Course titles (and content) which should make you wary

Words such as 'Total' and 'Dynamic' in the title of a course should make you look closely. Such buzz-words are sometimes used to make a course look different – or better – when in fact it is nothing out of the ordinary.

Be cautious then of titles like:

'Dynamic selling skills'
'Pro-active selling'
'Customer interactive techniques'
'Creating a total strategy for sales'

All of these could be straightforward selling technique courses dressed up. The content could be good sound stuff but in some cases it is not. The tendency to boost the course with a pseudo-management title is often accompanied by a lot of hype and not much substance in the course itself.

One such course is conducted in showman style over two days, accompanied by music and lights. A cross between a disco and the Nuremberg rally, the guts of the course could be put across in two or three hours at a fraction of the cost to the customer.

Entertainment or training?

Courses with musical back-up and fast-talking trainers can be very entertaining. They are rarely dull and the trainees will probably leave feeling thoroughly stimulated. They will also be inclined to write glowing letters of commendation which the company giving the course will print in its brochure.

This is all very fine but the important question to be asked is 'what have the trainees *learned*?'.

It certainly helps if a training course is lively and entertaining (it should not be dull) but the end result should be something learned rather than just an enjoyable day away from work.

Look closely at brochures and the like and ask yourself these questions:

- Do I understand the terms used?
- Is there a clearly stated objective which describes what the trainees will be able to do or understand at the end of the course?
- Is there a straightforward, understandable list of the course contents?
- Are the backgrounds and qualifications of the trainers described? If so, are they relevant to your employees?
- Does the brochure suggest the types of people for whom the course is suitable? In other words whether or not it is aimed at beginners, middle levels, specialists or other groups?

If you answer 'no' to any of these questions it is likely that the course is not for you.

Lots of impressive names

You may find that the brochure lists an impressive array of blue-chip companies who have used the course. This *could* indicate a high-quality course. It could also merely indicate that a big name company has used the course – once.

Don't assume that because Monster Consolidated International Inc. have used the course that it is any good or any good to you. You must check it out.

Checking it out

Having read the brochures and identified some courses which you feel might meet your needs some investigation should follow:

(1) *Contact the company offering the course and ask them to send you some samples of the course material.*
This, usually in the form of handouts, will enable you to assess the level and quality of the course and also to see if it is tailor-made for local (i.e. national) consumption. Many courses use materials developed in other countries, reflecting the style and terminology of those countries. Such imported products may not be particularly useful – particularly in cases such as sales training where local cultural and social differences can be crucial in the selection of the right techniques.

If the company concerned is reluctant to let you see its product – possibly making the silly excuse that copyright precludes it – give it a wide berth. Anyone offering a product or service should be willing to let potential customers take the pig out of the poke.

(2) *Take up some references.*
Have a word with other people who have used the course. The supplying company should be willing to give you the names of referees but if it will not forget it and look elsewhere.

(3) *Send one person on the course to make a first-hand assessment of its value to you.*
This will cost you some money so naturally you will only do it if you are happy with references and other information you have gleaned. It is also only worth doing if you can foresee the need to send a fair number of people on the course in future.

It is sometimes possible to persuade the supplying company to let one of your people sit in on the last two hours of a course – free of charge. This can be a good test as the attitude of the trainees to the course will be well established. Their demeanour can be observed and the opportunity taken to buttonhole one or two on the way out to find out what they think of the course.

What about the trainers?
It is important that the trainers have sufficient experience both of training itself and business in general to do a good job. They may, if the subject is a specialist one, need to have detailed specialist knowledge and hands-on experience. It may be helpful too if they have knowledge of your industry and its peculiarities, but this is not absolutely essential in most cases. It is often the principles and concepts of a subject which are needed and you should, in any case, be able and willing to 'interpret' these to fit them to the needs and circumstances of your own company.

Ask for details of the experience of the trainers and satisfy yourself that it is likely to be adequate for the job.

A warning about copyright.
Companies occasionally send one person on a course, not to

check it out, but to collect the material offered. This material is then photocopied and the trainee teaches his colleagues. Apart from any ethical question, this practice is illegal if the copyright to the material is infringed.

This method of trying to get some cheap training also has a high failure rate since the person sent on the course (unless a practised trainer himself) will not normally find it easy to duplicate the course.

SUMMARY OF KEY POINTS

1. There are positive benefits – in appropriate cases and with the right course – in using external training courses.

2. The benefits can include stimulating new ideas and stimulated people.

3. External courses are indicated:
- As part of exposure training
- When 'new blood' thinking is needed
- When attitudes need to be changed

4. There are many courses available ranging from one and two day seminars to a number of weeks.
   Choosing the right one is aided by referring to a responsible body such as a trade association.

5. Be sure that you understand what the course is all about – the title may mislead you.
   Look closely at courses with fancy titles full of 'totally dynamic positive interactive' buzz-words.

6. Check that the objective of the course is clear, the contents listed, the trainers right for the job and that the course is designed for your type of trainee.

7. Check the course out by examining sample handouts, taking up references and possibly, sending one person on the course to sample it.

CHAPTER SEVEN

The Training Budget

Is a budget really necessary?

The short answer is a very positive 'yes'. The absence of a training budget in some companies is a sign not that they do not need – or are not planning – any training but rather that they fail to include training as a serious part of company planning.

Budgets are often prepared to cover such vital activities as research and development, promotional schemes, purchase of new equipment and other influences on the future success and profitability of the business. Training, despite the equal importance it may have on the future ability to compete, has no budget. If and when it is realized that some training is necessary there is much wailing and gnashing of teeth as managers look around to see where the funds can come from. Something has to give and pinching some funds from the advertising budget or elsewhere not only causes the marketing people some headaches but does nothing to encourage their enthusiasm for training.

Nothing in – nothing out

A service industry company decided to computerize a number of its office activities. Executives and others were to be supplied with personal computers linked on a network. Access would be given to a mainframe data-base and a number of other facilities would be provided. These included electronic mail, telex preparation and transmission and expensively-developed special programmes for various individuals.

All this cost a substantial sum of money, took many months to put in place and was a key development in improving efficiency. The scheme was expected not only to give the company a clear edge on its competitors but also to reduce costs.

What happened?

The hardware was installed, programs were tested and then a long period of chaos and disillusionment began. The reason was that although a small fortune was spent on the scheme, training the users was virtually ignored. No training budget was provided since it was believed that an existing in-house computer specialist could do the training. This unfortunate man was able to provide only the barest and briefest instructions to the many people affected – who included not only the people who were to use the PCs but those who worked around them and whose jobs were also changed by the new system.

Some people learned quickly, some more slowly. All were expected to be up and running after their brief instruction session and, since this was not achieved, much of the benefit of the scheme was lost.

Had a budget for the training side of the scheme been insisted on *it would have drawn attention to what was needed.* An effective training plan would have been worked out and the chances are that the computerization scheme would have paid off as expected. Possibly the most valuable result of working out a budget for training (or anything else) is the fact that management attention must be paid to the subject. This increases the likelihood that the subject will be properly handled.

How much should your training budget be?

The first thing *not* to do is to follow the common practice of choosing a percentage of your payroll costs. This practice, normally resulting in a training budget of somewhere between one and three per cent of total payroll costs, is not only illogical but can cause a company to spend more than it need!

Choosing a percentage figure is another way of saying – 'We have accepted the idea that training is a 'Good Thing', we have to set some money aside for it but we have not a clue how much it ought to be'.

The budget for training should be arrived at after the same kind of analysis and planning which precedes the setting of a budget for anything else the company wants to do. One company decides its budget (on a percentage basis) after telephoning other companies to ask them what their percentages were. The relevance of someone else's budget to your own company needs is difficult to see and if, as is likely, the other companies have in turn set their budgets on the basis of someone else's figure we have a classic case of the blind leading the blind.

The amount that a company plans to spend on training should be a figure calculated after an assessment of training needs – which in turn is influenced by opportunities for profit improvement.

Working it out

Your appraisal scheme can give you a good starting point for working out your training budget.

Each training requirement identified during appraisal sessions will be geared either to a weakness to be corrected or a strength to be exploited. Action on both can be reasonably expected to improve company performance.

Other pointers to what is required are:

■ Future projects the success of which will, at least in part, depend on new or additional skills. Such projects, if planned properly, will have their own budgets, with training forming a part
■ Areas where there is reason to believe that improvement in

performance is necessary. This can include a potentially very wide range of subjects such as:
- customer service and care
- machine operating
- reduction of wastage e.g. rejects
- safety
- cash-flow e.g. credit control and debt collection
- machine utilization and scheduling
- production control
- level of sales
- stock control
- paperwork of one kind or another
■ Individuals who are in line for promotion or otherwise expected to take on more or wider responsibilities

There is no substitute for listing all the training needs, by individuals, if there is to be any real precision in your training budget. The listing and initial costing can be conveniently done on a worksheet such as this:

Training budget worksheet		Budget period: 1992	
Name	Subject	Course	Estimated cost £
Jones	Production planning	Acme college 5 days	750
Smith	French	Lingo training school 4 weeks	2,000
Bloggs	Credit control	OJT	20

Such a worksheet can be built up from the training plan illustrated in Chapter 2 and, if required, checked against the appraisal reports shown in Chapter 3.

The costs of in-house D.I.Y. training will of course include the cost of your trainer's time, and all forms of training will include the cost of the trainee's time. However, it is normally only necessary to list on the worksheet the out-of-pocket expenses. The time of employees will be included in the payroll budget.

The budget may also need to include such items as:

- Books
- Videos and audiotapes
- Hire of conference rooms
- Purchase or hire of projection and similar equipment
- Consultancy fees
- External trainer's fees

The listed costs can be added up on the worksheet to give a grand total which now goes into the budget melting-pot. Training needs and costs will now be reviewed against all the other demands to be made on the company's financial resources for the period concerned. The training budget may need to be trimmed and may be sent back to the originators for a re-think.

This process is no different from that imposed on every other company activity and should result in an approved amount of money which, in the context of the corporate picture, gives the best value for money with a clear result in mind.

The resulting amount has the merits that:

- It is based on analysis and not an arbitrary percentage
- It may be *less* than the arbitrary percentage – but if greater it is at least based on the facts
- Managers will know exactly what the money is to be spent on and not left to hunt around for some training simply because they have some money available

It sometimes happens that managers, finding that they still

have some money left over from the percentage-based budget and realizing that the budget period is nearly over, spend it. This is done to avoid a cut in the budget for the next period as a result of this year's budget not being fully used. This is clearly nonsensical and is bad for profits. A detail-based training budget helps to avoid it.

The ha'p'orth of tar trap

A company trainer *having obtained agreement* and a budget for a 12-month training plan was approached by the personnel director. 'Can you cut your expenditure in any way?' the director asked. The trainer was unable to suggest any significant cuts and, since the budget had been agreed after a detailed analysis, was reluctant to do so. Every penny of expenditure was justified by a calculated purpose, and all the training agreed could be shown to contribute to the company future in a specific way.

The personnel director, probably under some pressure from his peers, then suggested that certain courses could be reduced in duration – thus reducing hire charges for conference rooms. He further suggested doing without certain training videos, notwithstanding the fact that they were part of carefully constructed courses.

Despite the trainer's protests, these cuts were made, with the result that the courses were incomplete and rushed. The objectives were not achieved in the case of all the trainees which meant that for the sake of some cheeseparing a lot of time and money was wasted.

Don't put your company at risk by cheeseparing.

Some more dos and don'ts

■ *Do provide the trainer with all he needs in the way of kits, visual aids and the like.* Depriving him of the tools of his trade is like refusing petrol to a delivery driver.

■ *Don't press for courses to be reduced (or abandoned) because you cannot spare people to go on the course.* This is just a way of scrapping training altogether and prolonging any lack of skills you suffer from. There is never a time 'when we are less busy', so bite the bullet when you said you would.

■ *Do provide a proper training room and some reasonable comfort for your trainees.* People learn better in an hotel conference room than in a cramped little corner of your factory or a draughty hut.

■ *Don't necessarily choose the cheapest courses* – they may not be the best value for money. The course you should pay for is the one with the right content and provided by people you have checked out.

Conversely don't imagine that because a course is massively expensive it must be the best. It could be more hype and five-star accommodation than substance.

■ *Don't be mean about travelling expenses, refreshments and perks.* They can all contribute to a sense of enjoyment of the training – which encourages learning.

■ *Don't try to save money by making people work late into the night.* This macho approach is often self-defeating simply because tired people do not easily learn.

N.B. There is something to be gained if syndicate exercises and the like are carried out in the evenings – providing that it is *genuinely* voluntary with no come-back if the work is not done. If the atmosphere is right and the motivation effective most people *will* do such work. No-one however wants to be back in the classroom late at night for yet another lecture (from a tired lecturer).

Checking for value for money

Any complete and properly-designed budgeting system will have a facility for checking expenditure against the budget agreed. Actual expenditure will be compared, probably monthly, with the budget figure, and 'variances' reported. In most cases the rate of expenditure will be translated into an annualized figure to forecast what the year's outcome will be if expenditure continues at the rate recorded to date. This type of control is as essential in training budgets as it is with budgets for anything else. There is, though, more that should be done in respect of training expenses to see what return is being enjoyed for the money spent. If, as it should be, training is regarded as an investment then the 'dividend' should be measured. If this is not done training will come to be regarded as a 'cost-centre' only and will be the first casualty when ways are sought to reduce expenditure in future.

In addition, measurement of the dividend can point to the training (and the methods used) with a big pay-off and highlight the less successful training where results have been disappointing. The results achieved and measured can be used to show where it is advantageous to:

■ Fine-tune successful training
■ Step up or expand successful courses
■ Amend methods which are less than satisfactory
■ Scrap courses or methods which have a poor pay-off
■ Identify and re-train trainees who have not achieved all they could

Measuring the dividend

Some imagination will be needed in finding reliable ways to measure the results and value of your training. Post-course questionnaires will give some indication but, since the answers given will be to a great extent subjective, something else will be needed.

The acid test is likely to be something which is:

■ Easily measured, e.g. you will not have to set up some new and elaborate recording system

- Influential on profit either directly or indirectly – and if indirectly, in an obvious way
- Not partly attributable to some other influence, e.g. seasonal factors, price changes or competitors' actions. In other words, whatever result is being measured can, with reasonable certainty, be attributed only to the training.

Possible dividends to be measured might include:

- Sales levels e.g. after sales technique training or refresher courses in the features and benefits of company products
- Output levels e.g. after machine operating training or the introduction of new production planning methods
- Frequency of errors e.g. in invoicing, costing or order entry after the training of clerical staff in basic procedures
- Reject levels on a production line e.g. after machine-operator training
- Number of customer complaints e.g. after training of retail sales assistants, despatch staff, quality control staff and the like.

Any substantial improvements after training, in results such as these, should be evaluated. Let us suppose for example that you spent £5,000 on training part of your sales team. If, after the training, sales increased so that profits were improved by £20,000 per annum then you know that the training was a first-class investment, probably worth repeating and a justification of your original budget.

If, at the same time as the re-trained sales people were launched into the market, you kicked off a new advertising campaign or introduced an improved product, then it could be difficult, to say the least, to attribute any hike in sales to the training alone.

Customer complaints and error reduction also need careful handling since they are not always so easy to 'price'. One company priced its customer complaints by assuming that, on average, each one required two hour's clerical effort and one hour's management effort to put right. These figures were based on examining a number of actual cases and were not just a guess. A cost of £20 per hour was attributed to clerical time and £40 per hour to management time.

It was thus calculated that the average complaint cost about £80 to put right – with no figure being attributed to damage to the company reputation.

The training cost was easy to calculate and a comparison of the number of complaints before and after training was carried out. The training was shown on this basis to be a financial success, although one senior manager claimed that the improvement was not due to the training but to 'the fact that staff were now more aware of the cost of customer complaints'.

This was true – and the cost of complaints was a heavily-emphasized point made to the trainees during their training sessions!

Something you could not do before the training

There are a number of situations – the introduction of a computer system is a frequently occurring one – where something could not be done at all without the training which was required. The value in the training cannot in most cases be isolated from the value of the whole package but it is nevertheless there.

In a not untypical case a computer system for accounting purposes cost £5,150. The training cost, included in this figure, was £550. Without this training expenditure the system could not have been operated at all so the value, although not capable of being expressed in cash terms, is more or less clear.

A reminder about the ha'p'orth of tar

Management, when considering the training budget for a project where training value cannot be expressed in cash terms, should avoid trying to prune it beyond the point where the value of the whole project is endangered. Such a mistake is not uncommon – often because the importance of the training to the project is not fully appreciated. Attention tends to be focused on the more exciting aspects such as impressive new equipment or promotional campaigns.

SUMMARY OF KEY POINTS

1. Training costs should be budgeted in the same way as every other company expense.

2. If training is an essential part of any project or company development the lack of a budget can endanger the success of the whole scheme.

3. Working out the budget draws attention to the part training will play in company activities and increases the chances that it will be properly (and economically) handled.

4. *Don't* decide the training budget on the basis of a percentage of payroll or other arbitrary figure. This is illogical and can waste money. The training budget should be worked out on the basis of actual costs to meet an agreed need.

5. Work out your budget by looking at the detail – and by using a worksheet.

6. Don't forget all the 'extras' such as video hire and books.

7. Be careful not to spoil your training ship for the lack of a ha'p'orth of tar.
    Training on the cheap is not likely to succeed.

8. Don't be mean about travelling expenses. Don't try to cut costs by making exhausted people work late into the night and don't automatically choose the cheapest course available.

9. Check for value for money. Measure, as far as possible, the results of your training and its impact on profits.

APPENDIX I

Making Your Own Training Video

It is most likely that you will, in practice, need to have your own training video made for you.

A really effective video is not likely to result from the work of an enthusiastic amateur and unless you have a trained producer *and team* on your staff you really should commission an outside expert.

It is not uncommon when a company video is mentioned to find one or more would-be Cecil B. De Milles emerging from the ranks of the staff. These are often the people who bought a video camera for use on last summer's family holiday and now feel themselves to be God's Gift To Hollywood. The holiday shots may have been wonderful and full of interest to Grannie and old Uncle George but this does not mean that the camera owner can produce a training video.

Beware also the 'actors' who will offer their services and the chief executive who insists on an introductory talk (by him). The person who was a 'wow' in school amateur dramatics will not necessarily come over well in a video. A ten-minute preamble from the chairman is also likely to be a disaster – the hypnotic effect of his head and shoulders telling the audience how committed he is to training and exhorting the trainees to greater efforts will probably send everyone to sleep.

Why have your own video?

There are many ready made and excellent training videos already on the market so why have one specially made for you?

It is most unlikely that anyone has made a video covering

either your company or the particular part of your organization where training is needed.

One well-known company with many retail branches had worries about security. A number of robberies had taken place in their branches and it was realized that many of them could have been prevented if branch managers had taken some simple precautions. No video existed which covered the particular precautions needed so it was decided to commission one to meet the specific needs of the company. The result was a training programme which:

- Dealt only with the particular security needs of the company
- Would be meaningful to employees as it covered activities which were part of their daily lives and familiar to them
- Involved established company procedures concerning branch administration, banking cash and the like

In other words the trainees could relate to the video's message which was recognizably dealing with *their* jobs and *their* activities. A general video on security might have been available off the shelf but it is likely that much of it would have been irrelevant or would need translation of its message into practical terms for the company concerned. This translation is sometimes a feasible proposition – but not always.

Another company decided that it needed its own video to cover some highly esoteric aspects of its activities. Unfortunately it decided to make the video itself. The result was a very boring 30 minutes of someone talking (in a rather dreary monotone) and filmed by a hand held camera. The most absorbing part of the video was the wobbling about of the camera although some people were entertained by counting the lengthy pauses as the talker consulted his notes.

Finding someone to do the job for you

There are many companies in the business of making videos – good, bad and indifferent. It is obviously important to pick a good one.

A useful starting point is The International Visual Communications Association (102, Great Russell Street, London WC1E 3LN. Tel: 071–580 0962). The IVCA is a non-profit making organization representing, amongst others, video production companies and suppliers of hardware and services. The Association, which has a working party on good practice, can provide you with a list of members who may be able to meet your needs.

Otherwise you might refer to industry guides such as Kemps International Film and Television Year Book.

Having obtained a few names of potential people to choose from what do you need to look for?

Making your choice

Perhaps the first thing to consider is the people. You will meet representatives of the producing company – a 'must' is to meet the actual person who would be responsible for making your video – and this will give you the chance to check out a number of important points viz:

■ Can you see yourself working comfortably with these people? Your staff may have to spend many hours with them; will they get along?

■ How much and what sort of experience do the people have – particularly the intended producer? The experience should be relevant e.g. in making training videos as opposed to, say, sales videos

■ Are they used to working with companies of your size and with your level of resources? They may have a number of prestigious clients but are you in the same league? If not, it does not necessarily mean that they will do a poor job for you but they may expect more from you in terms of, say, time of your staff than you can manage

- How much care do they take in finding out what your needs are? Are they willing to spend some time (unpaid) asking questions and listening carefully to your answers? In short, do they show real concern for the customer?

If you are happy with the people and their attitude to you the next step is to get some ideas of the quality of their work – once again and in particular the work of the producer who will be making your video.

- Ask to see a 'show-reel' of excerpts of previous work
- Look at a complete programme. How does it score on such subjects as pace, style, clarity of narration?
  If you see a previously made training video judge how easily you can learn from it
- Ask for the names of previous clients to whom you can refer – and ask these clients how well their video performed in practice.

Let's suppose that you are suitably impressed by the quality of the work that you have seen.

You now need to consider whether the producing company has the resources necessary to handle your project.

Ask for evidence of financial stability and probe the way in which they manage their business. Don't be shy about this as you too will have to commit quite a lot of time and effort into the production and if the producer runs out of cash before the job is done it could be costly.

Check what facilities they have – equipment, people, space and so on. They may hire equipment, studios, vehicles and other items and this is not in itself necessarily a bad thing. They may use hiring as a sensible means to hold down overhead costs but you must be sure that they have the cash flow to pay the hire charges.

N.B. Don't be put off by the fact that a potential supplier is small. The quality of the people and the work they produce is not governed by the size of the operation. The smaller companies may try harder and, if you are small too, may give you more attention than a large company which gets most of its business from the really big boys.

You have chosen your producer – what next?

You will, when in the process of choosing your producer, have decided with him your objectives – even if only in general terms.

Having chosen your producer it is essential that your objective is turned into a full and detailed brief. This brief will fulfil the following functions:

- It provides the producer with a clear statement of what is wanted and its purpose. This acts as a starting-point for the producer's work e.g. planning the programme
- It provides a mechanism to ensure that you have thought the purpose through and acts as a means to communicate the idea to all concerned
- It will confirm such points as the target audience, what are the key messages to be put across and how you expect the video to influence the audience

Following the brief the producer will work out what has to be done, by whom, when and where and should discuss with you various possibilities and alternatives. Resulting from this should be a budget and a contract.

If both of these are acceptable to both you and the producer the actual production work can start. This may include research both on and off your premises and will include working out a production schedule. A script will be needed and various arrangements will be made for work on location.

Ultimately filming will start and in due course you will be able to view a first version (termed an off-line edit) prior to final editing.

Working with the producer

The whole process of making an effective video requires specialist skills. Producers and their teams exist to provide those skills. The commissioning company, having signed the contract, should be guided by the producer and allow him to get on with the job.

It is not unknown for a poor result to be achieved as a result of the commissioning company telling the producer what to do.

The following errors are all real situations and indicate the dos and don'ts:

- The chairman who insisted on amending the script and re-writing it himself. The result was not only a very boring and barely comprehensible voice-over but it allowed no visual action. The audience had to look at the same objects for minutes on end.
- The company who formed a committee of eight people to liaise with the producer. Several members of the committee tried to 'call the shots' and the producer was given conflicting information. The muddle was such that the whole process had to be re-started when the company was persuaded to appoint *one* person to liaise with the producer and his team.
- The company which repeatedly changed its mind as work progressed. The effect of a number of new briefs was a job which ran hugely over budget.
- The senior executive who prided himself on his knowledge of music and insisted on choosing background themes from works which had not been 'rights cleared'. This meant that

substantial fees had to be paid to use the music – which many felt was in any case inappropriate.

The golden rule is 'be guided by your professional adviser – the producer'.

What about the cost?
Making a video is not cheap. In addition to the producer the team will consist (at least) of cameraman, sound recordist and an assistant. There will be transport costs, insurances, some pricey equipment and, possibly, the hire of an actor for visual roles or voice-over. It is unlikely that costs will be less than £10,000 and the sky is the limit at the other end of the scale.

However, before your accountant throws a fit put the cost in perspective. Ask what result you expect for your money. Suppose for example you pay £20,000 for a video and use it to train 20 factory operatives, what can you expect for £1,000 per operative? It could result in waste reduction more than equal to £1,000 per operative over say 12 months. If the same sum is spent to train ten salesmen (i.e. £2,000 each) and each one brings in additional orders worth £20,000, with a profit margin of 10 per cent the video is paid for. From then on the video is, in effect, making a profit.

More detailed information
Further and fairly detailed advice on how to go about commissioning a video is contained in a booklet entitled *Commissioning a Programme*, published by The International Visual Communication Association.

The booklet includes a draft agreement for use by producer and client and a useful glossary of terms used in the video world. Particularly helpful are some checklists of various costs and fees which can assist in working out a budget.

APPENDIX II

Some Kits to Help You

Perhaps the simplest kit you can use is the ready-made videotape. These are normally provided with a booklet offering suggestions as to how to use the video – for example as the basis for group discussion on the subjects covered. Most of the videos on the market run for about 20 minutes and, with the help of the guiding notes in the booklet, can form the centre-piece to a session of about one hour.

A lot can be learned in a short time from these simple kits which can be used by relatively inexperienced trainers. The visual impact of a video is equivalent to a lot of words either heard or read and the good ones reduce apparently complicated subjects to the essential points very effectively.

A little more sophistication

A stage further on from the 'video plus notes' level are training packages which add other media to the video. These additions can include audio tapes, slides and written material.

An example of such a package is one of a number marketed by Longman Training (formerly Rank Training).

Longman (Cullum House, North Orbital Road, Denham, Uxbridge UB9 5HL, Tel: 0895 834142) offer a package entitled *Getting the Business and Keeping it*.

This is an in-house sales training course comprising:

- A course teacher's manual
- A Leader's guide – a detailed script for running the course
- 8 Video tapes
- Overhead transparencies
- Pre-course reading – to prepare the trainees for the course

- Memory Aid Cards – reminders of the essential points
- Post-course reading

The course itself is made up of 5 modules with a video sequence for each one.

The in-house advantage

One of the benefits of packages such as this is that, unlike courses taken 'out-of-house', the material can be used as appropriate to the company and the people involved. The user company also has the choice of when to hold the course and, if they wish, to hold it in a number of short sessions. This flexibility can be very helpful when there are difficulties in withdrawing busy staff from their day to day activities.

Computer-based training systems

There are two types of computer-based systems. The simplest is known as 'Computer Based Training' (CBT) in which computer-generated images are stored on a floppy disk. The disks can be read using a computer terminal.

The second and more sophisticated type of system is the so-called 'Interactive Video' (I.V.) which combines images stored on a laser disc with the power of a computer. The result is a system which can ask questions of the trainee as well as provide information. These systems work on a one-to-one basis.

The trainee works at his own pace and learns by mistakes or wrong decisions as well as by absorbing the information given. The confidence of the trainee is maintained by the fact that his errors are apparent only to himself. However, some kits can produce a printout to show the trainee's progress and to facilitate help from a tutor.

Longman Training is a leading supplier of this type of system. Among the subjects covered by the Longman kits are:

- Assertiveness

- Customer relations
- Delegation skills
- Stress at work
- Time management
- Teamwork
- Negotiating skills

Hands-on and work-based

A leading supplier of kits with a difference is Macmillan Intek Limited, Intek House, Ellen Street, Hove BN3 3XL (Tel: 0273 21564).

Macmillan Intek, which has associates and distributors in Europe, Australia and New Zealand, supplies 'skill training programmes' using some or all of videos, audio tapes, workbooks and computer disks. It adds to these, in appropriate cases, practical simulation kits.

Suppose, for example, you wish to train someone in basic electrical skills. The Macmillan Intek kits for this subject include electrical components with which the trainee can put the theory into practice with hands-on exercises.

At the end of the training the trainee should, amongst other things, be able to make voltage measurements, check the power rating of a resistor and make measurements in a series resistor circuit.

Such packages are accredited by City and Guilds and BTEC and can be linked to other packages in the range. Combinations of packages can be used to provide a complete skills programme directly appropriate to the trainee's job.

The Macmillan Intek range includes:

- Tools, soldering and test instruments
- Electronics (e.g. digital devices)
- Microprocessor architecture and fault-finding
- Lathe and milling machine operating techniques
- Data communication

First Line Management skills are also included in the Macmillan Intek range. An action-based programme that takes place in the workplace links company and departmental objectives to the self-development of the individual. A work based project forms part of the learning and acts as an assessment process.

The FLM programme covers company objectives, management of human and other resources, how effectively to identify and solve problems – and how to carry out an improvement project. This package is endorsed by the Management Charter Initiative and on successful completion enables the trainee to be awarded the BTEC certificate in management studies.

In addition to these off-the-shelf packages, Macmillan Intek can provide tailor-made programmes designed to address the specific needs of your company and its people.

Choosing the Place for Your Training

Deciding on the place to hold your training courses (assuming that they are not being held in-house) involves far more than simply 'phoning an hotel or conference centre in a convenient spot.

The nature of the place you choose can make a big difference to the quality of your training – for good or ill. You can also spend more money than is necessary and still find the result less than satisfactory. There is, for example, a large and expensive hotel in London offering large and expensive rooms for conferences and training. The rooms are well decorated and the furniture is fine. Unfortunately the rooms are full of pillars and the acoustics are dreadful. The result is that quite a lot of people cannot see the speaker or the screen or other equipment, and the ones at the back cannot hear anything.

Teaching in these conditions is extremely difficult and learning is inhibited. What then, should we look for?

The following checklist covers all the essentials:

(1) *The size and shape of the room.*
If the room is too large the trainees will feel lost in it. If too small it will feel cramped and claustrophobic. The ideal size will depend on how you intend to seat your people and there are a number of choices, viz:

■ *Classroom style.* Each trainee should have a minimum of three feet of clear desk or table space in front of him and enough space behind him to push back his chair and stretch out his legs. It is uncomfortable to be constantly crouched over a desk or to be elbow to elbow with adjacent people.

- *Boardroom style.* A similar amount of space per trainee is needed as for the classroom style. In addition, the 'boardroom table' should be wide enough to avoid trainees having to stare across it into each other's eyes or to have to turn uncomfortably to see the trainer. Space to push back the chairs is again important.
- *Horseshoe shape.* This is a good shape for encouraging discussion and general participation as it allows everyone to see everyone else and also the speaker. A distance of not less than ten feet should be allowed between the arms of the horseshoe.

The shape of the room should permit your chosen arrangement and should also allow for everyone to see any visual aid you intend to use. Long, narrow rooms tend to create difficulties as of course do any pillars or other obstructions.

(2) *The position and nature of power points.*
You can bet your boots that unless you check it the only power point in the room will be either too far away for the projector lead to reach it, will not fit your plug or will not work at all.

(3) *Lighting.*
Too many conference rooms have too little light and in two or three hours your trainees will develop headaches. Ideally the level of lighting will be adjustable and it will include some natural light.

(4) *Acoustics.*
Test the room for echoes and 'dead spots'. These problems normally only occur in very large rooms but it is still worth checking. The speaker should be clearly audible in every part of the room when speaking in a firm voice but without strain.

(5) *Distractions.*
Check that there are no internal or external noises which will

trouble you. These can include aircraft noise (airport hotels), school playgrounds, lorries thundering by, the hotel kitchens, building works and the wedding party in the next room.

Other forms of distraction include:

■ Uncomfortable chairs − try them out
■ Room too hot or too cold − ideally you will be able to control the temperature
■ Poor ventilation
■ Kitchen or other smells

(6) *Facilities for breaks.*
The room should have enough space for tea, coffee etc. to be served away from the working area. A table in a corner or elsewhere should allow for the trainees to collect their refreshments and walk about. This provides a welcome physical and mental break.

There should also be some provision for a change of scene and a little exercise during lunch or other long breaks. A pleasant garden allowing a stroll or a putting green are ideal. Best of all is a leisure area with a swimming pool and exercise room where the trainees can work off some calories and re-charge the mental batteries.

(7) *Meals.*
A buffet arrangement is best for midday meals as serving time is much shorter. The trainees should be able to eat in comfort and then have a little time to take a stroll or otherwise relax before returning to the classroom. Waiter or waitress service may be fine for evening meals but generally takes too long during the day.

(8) *What you get for the price.*
Most hotels and conference centres will quote an all-in price. This will cover the conference room, meals and any overnight

accommodation. Watch out though for 'extras' such as a charge for supplying a video player or overhead projector. Such extras are sometimes *very* expensive. Try to negotiate a deal covering *everything* – or bring your own bits and pieces.

(9) *Syndicate areas.*
You may include in your training some exercises or other work to be done in 'syndicates' by groups of trainees. Check that there are suitable places for this work to be done such as corners of bars and lounges which are not too busy mid-morning and mid-afternoon.

Allow for Murphy's Law

Something will go wrong so be prepared. The following survival kit is recommended:

- Spare bulbs and fuses for electrical equipment
- An extension lead for your projector, a spare plug and a screwdriver
- Spare flip chart pens – the ones you are given may be dried out
- Sellotape and Blu-tack for fixing flip chart sheets to walls
- Pads of paper – the hotel pads will consist of only three or four pages
- Pain killers and Alka-Seltzer – some fool will overdo it in the bar

Finally, at least an hour before you start, check everything:

- Does the video work?
- Can you focus the projector?
- Is the power point supplying power?
- Are there enough chairs?

and so on.

A Special Word on Computer Training

Training your staff in the use of computers is not merely a matter of teaching them how to use the keyboards and other hardware forming part of the system.

If you are introducing computers for the first time or bringing in a new or more sophisticated system then future success will depend heavily on other factors.

Managers in particular need to understand:

- *How the existence of the system can affect the company as a whole.* The system may, for example, provide information which was either not available before or was very slow in coming. The information could significantly change the way in which decisions are taken and when. Opportunities for improved working methods may present themselves – for example by being able to work with lower stock levels.
- *The discipline which may have to be observed.* Computers are unforgiving of mistakes and unless there is a built-in screening process, garbage in will result in garbage out. Computers, unlike human beings, will not correct the errors made by someone further down the line or rectify errors of omission.

Where in the past clerk A may have corrected the errors of clerk B before passing on a document the computer will not do this. Clerk B therefore must get it right and no longer depend on clerk A.

If the computer is programmed to reject transactions which are incorrect or incomplete then referrals back and delays will occur.

This will not, as is often alleged, be due to a 'computer

error' but to a human error and lack of working discipline – which is a subject which people need to be taught.

■ *The length of time to write or re-write a programme – and why.* Once the computer system is installed it will not be possible to make much in the way of short term changes – something of which some managements are over-fond.

■ *The effects of the system throughout the company.* In addition to the increased need to observe disciplines, the system is likely to speed up various operations. This can mean re-arranging long established work programmes. In addition, since data may be readily available from the computer system, the old filing systems or record books may no longer be needed. All this means that the people affected must be re-trained. If this is not done much of the benefits of a computer system can be lost. In the worst cases an old manual system is expensively retained 'behind the scenes' and will conflict with the computer system

A broad understanding of computers and computing is required at management level (even by people not directly using the system) if full benefits are to be obtained. Only rarely, it seems, do senior people obtain this knowledge – leaving themselves heavily dependent on a few relatively junior people to keep the company process going. In some cases these junior people can effectively decide how the company will go about many aspects of the company's business simply because the proper decision makers don't understand how it all works.

There are, in addition, some essential guidelines for training the hands-on users of the system.

Don't underestimate how much training is needed
Some people take to computing with ease. Others find it frightening and difficult to understand.

You may be tempted to believe that the one day course proposed by 'Super Dooper PC Trainers Ltd.' is good enough to meet the need. This is unlikely to be the case for all your staff. Allowance should be made in the implementation timetable and the budget for substantial repeat training.

Train in small groups

Ideally the use of computer equipment will be taught on a one-to-one basis. At most one-to-three is the limit. Attempts to train a large group are unlikely to succeed as there is normally much small detail to cover which individuals will find more or less difficult to absorb and remember.

Keyboard use, the selection of 'screens', and alternative ways to use the system need concentrated attention and individual explanation.

Allow for lots of practice

Ample practice (e.g. on keyboards) is required *before* the system goes live. It is a big mistake to believe that immediately the formal training is completed employees will be able to swing into action with the accuracy and speed which you are hoping for. Errors will occur, equipment mysteriously cease to function and the wrong buttons will be pressed.

Practice is needed in dealing with these mini-disasters and not just the overall nuts and bolts of the system.

Support for the turn-key package

There are companies who will provide you with a computer system on a turn-key basis. That is they will design the system for you, install the hardware and software and train your staff.

This arrangement can work well but an 'extension' to the training in the form of a help-line is something you should insist on. This service, a 24-hour 'phone-in for help, is provided by many suppliers as part of the deal. This is a valuable form of support which should be available for three months or so. It is a fact that the great majority of problems are caused by simple and basic errors which, while potentially devastating to the system, can be cleared up in a few minutes on the telephone. It is not unknown, for example, for the person on the end of the help-line to find that the customer who cannot get his computer to print something has failed to switch his printer on!

A way to do some all-round training

A relatively inexpensive way to do some all-round background training – to ensure that everyone understands how your new computer system can affect the business – is to use one or more of a series of videos produced by the *Sunday Times*.

At the time of writing there are 18 videos in the series covering the following subjects:

- Computer Aided Design
- Word Processing
- Spreadsheets
- Accounts
- Databases
- Communications
- Desktop Publishing
- Choosing a micro
- Networks
- Teleworking

An appropriate selection of these videos could be shown to your staff, including directors and senior managers. They will not, as a result, become experts on computer systems but they will gain a good all-round knowledge of some of the principles and concepts. This will better enable them to see how they and their colleagues may be affected even if they are not directly involved. They will also be better able to appreciate what is being done and why.

The videos can be obtained from:

The Sunday Times Video Library, PO Box 169, Horsham, West Sussex. Fax: 0403 61555.

APPENDIX V

Ford's Employee Development and Assistance Programme

Ford Motor Company Limited launched, in 1989, its Employee Development and Assistance Programme.

The company's annual report for 1989 states that EDAP 'offers opportunities to all employees to receive up to £200 in grants in any one year to assist them in educational, training and health programmes'.

The scheme, believed to be the first of its kind in British industry, works through a joint employee and management committee and is supported by colleges and further education institutions.

A wide range of courses is available through the programme, providing employees with the opportunity for personal development, advancement and progression.

It is important to note that the training undertaken is not job-related. It is described in the company literature as being 'concerned with education, training and health and is separate from the Company's ongoing training programme'.

Some of the courses chosen by employees, whilst not part of the normal job training, are close enough in content to be of assistance in the job. Examples are the drivers of heavy goods vehicles who are learning German to make communications easier on cross-border trips. Similarly, a jetty driver has opted for an advanced driving course.

However, overall the programme is clearly designed to result in a better-educated (and healthier) workforce. Chosen courses include writing, social sciences, languages, photography, computer skills and health programmes.

Approval for courses is required and the company makes the point that wholly recreational courses such as windsurfing are not likely to be given backing. In addition, all courses must be taken outside working hours.

Does the company benefit?

The answer must be 'yes' in the medium- to long-term and providing the scheme is well administered. A better-educated workforce is likely to be a more effective workforce. Individuals introduced to new ideas and with wider interests are likely to be more lively and imaginative than those whose lives are limited to work and watching television. Time will tell how both Ford and its employees will benefit but the idea behind the scheme is clearly to be commended.

Will your employees benefit?

The answer must be 'yes' if only because they are doing something which they choose to do i.e. something they want to do.

There is also an industrial relations angle of considerable significance. The following comment was made by Mr. K.W. Mortimer of Ford:

'One of the reasons why Ford introduced the programme was that the experience of Unions working together with Management in local committees on a regular basis for the benefit of employees would lead to fostering a spirit of teamwork which would have obvious spin-offs in improving industrial relations. From my own research a number of Convenors and Personnel Managers are already attesting to the value of EDAP in improving industrial relations by developing teamwork'.

Is EDAP for big companies only?

Someone is bound to say 'This sort of thing is all very well for a huge and successful company like Ford. We are too small to be able to do anything similar'.

Why should this be so? The financial part of the scheme is limited to a fixed amount per course, so that the total cost to the company is determined by the number of employees involved. Ford may have the resources to subsidize hundreds of courses for hundreds of people but if you employ only a dozen people can you not find the funds to assist the dozen? You can, like Ford, credit your programme with £50 per employee. This is unlikely to break the bank.

Why not make a start by finding out what your local Adult Education centres can offer? Many courses will be much less expensive than £200 or even £50.

Then, talk to your employees. Find out how many will be prepared to put in the effort if you pay the fee.

You may find that for a modest expense training can be provided which will benefit the employees and contribute to the company future. Languages could be valuable if you are exporting (or planning to export) and with business technology moving apace almost any computer training is likely to pay off. Writing skills, arithmetic, assertiveness, investment, psychology, and health are all subjects commonly found at evening classes and all are likely to be of benefit. Fitness is another area worth considering – on the basis that fit people work better, take less sick-leave and feel better. A programme aimed at weight reduction and general physical improvement can also be of great value in combating stress – a hazard facing shop-floor workers quite as much as those in the boardroom.

APPENDIX VI

A Peep into the Future

For how long will training be heavily based on seminars and classrooms?

New technology is likely to take us beyond the classrooms and even the more sophisticated training kits available. Developments are being made in the use of satellite television – more particularly, at the time of writing, for training in certain professions.

BAe Communications is, for example, developing a television-based system to service post-graduate medical centres. It should be noted that these systems are not the same as the television programmes such as those for schools and the Open University with which we are all familiar. The idea involves interaction between the trainees and the presenters of the programmes by means of an audio link.

Similar ideas are in the pipeline for people in the legal profession and also for farmers.

While it is early days, with pilot programmes being run during 1991, forecasts have been made that the days of the seminar are numbered. This may or may not be the case but it is likely that this development will result in an additional choice of training method in the future.

Tele-working is already well-established and provides an example of how work can be done by individuals remote from a central point but in contact with it. The same principle applied to training could mean the use of electronic equipment to enable a number of people to 'attend a seminar' without leaving their homes or places of work.

It could pay you to keep in touch with developments such as this and to go for them if they suit your needs.

Some Further Sources of Information

Some additional reading which you might find useful is provided by:

Ideas for Enterprising Managers by Matthew Archer (Mercury: London 1988)
This book offers advice on appraisal schemes, setting up OJT, delegation and how to sell the idea of training in your company.

The Best Person for the Job by Malcolm Bird (Piatkus: London 1989)
This covers induction of new employees in some detail and also manpower planning for the smaller business.

Capital People (1980) by Amin Rajan
This is a report published by the Industrial Society which deals, among other relevant topics, with the future (and adverse) consequences of the failure of City firms to train their people.

Road Transport – The 90s Skills Gap (RTIB Publication, MOTEC High Ercall, Telford, Shropshire)
This will be of interest to people in the transport business – especially those looking ahead to staff and skill requirements in the early 1990s.

Management Mole by John Mole (Bantam Press, 1989)
This provides a fascinating account of managers and their actions as seen from the viewpoint of a temporary clerk.

Experiences in eleven companies are described – giving ample evidence of a massive need for management training – and why.

Performance Management 1990 (available from The Wyatt Company, 21 Tothill Street, London SW1)
This reports on the results of a survey into the views of personnel staff on their appraisal schemes.

The Learning Organisation by Bob Garratt (Fontana: London, 1987)
This deals with the role of directors and points out some ways in which they can prepare themselves for that role.

Expert System Opportunities (HMSO)
Published in both book and video form, this will be helpful if training people in the use of computer systems designed to be used repeatedly and consistently by a number of people. An example is the use by firms of accountants of an expert system to sort out clients' VAT queries without having to consult a VAT specialist.

Index